NATIONAL ACADEMIES Sciences Engineering Medicine

NATIONAL ACADEMIES PRESS
Washington, DC

Understanding and Offsetting Financial Barriers for Black Students in Science, Engineering, and Medicine

Programs, Partnerships, and Pathways

Gilda A. Barabino,
Theodore J. Corbin, Jr., and
Paula Whitacre, *Rapporteurs*

Cato T. Laurencin, *Editor*

Roundtable on Black Men and
Black Women in Science,
Engineering, and Medicine

Policy and Global Affairs

Health and Medicine Division

Proceedings of a Workshop

THE NATIONAL ACADEMIES PRESS 500 Fifth Street, NW Washington, DC 20001

This activity was supported by contracts between the National Academy of Sciences and the National Institutes of Health (HHSN263201800029I/75N98021F00006). Any opinions, findings, conclusions, or recommendations expressed in this publication do not necessarily reflect the views of any organization or agency that provided support for the project.

International Standard Book Number-13: 978-0-309-68889-5
International Standard Book Number-10: 0-309-68889-2
Digital Object Identifier: https://doi.org/10.17226/26576

This publication is available from the National Academies Press, 500 Fifth Street, NW, Keck 360, Washington, DC 20001; (800) 624-6242 or (202) 334-3313; http://www.nap.edu.

Printed in the United States of America.

Suggested citation: National Academies of Sciences, Engineering, and Medicine. 2022. *Understanding and Offsetting Financial Barriers for Black Students in Science, Engineering, and Medicine: Programs, Partnerships, and Pathways: Proceedings of a Workshop*. Washington, DC: The National Academies Press. https://doi.org/10.17226/26576.

The **National Academy of Sciences** was established in 1863 by an Act of Congress, signed by President Lincoln, as a private, nongovernmental institution to advise the nation on issues related to science and technology. Members are elected by their peers for outstanding contributions to research. Dr. Marcia McNutt is president.

The **National Academy of Engineering** was established in 1964 under the charter of the National Academy of Sciences to bring the practices of engineering to advising the nation. Members are elected by their peers for extraordinary contributions to engineering. Dr. John L. Anderson is president.

The **National Academy of Medicine** (formerly the Institute of Medicine) was established in 1970 under the charter of the National Academy of Sciences to advise the nation on medical and health issues. Members are elected by their peers for distinguished contributions to medicine and health. Dr. Victor J. Dzau is president.

The three Academies work together as the **National Academies of Sciences, Engineering, and Medicine** to provide independent, objective analysis and advice to the nation and conduct other activities to solve complex problems and inform public policy decisions. The National Academies also encourage education and research, recognize outstanding contributions to knowledge, and increase public understanding in matters of science, engineering, and medicine.

Learn more about the National Academies of Sciences, Engineering, and Medicine at **www.nationalacademies.org**.

Consensus Study Reports published by the National Academies of Sciences, Engineering, and Medicine document the evidence-based consensus on the study's statement of task by an authoring committee of experts. Reports typically include findings, conclusions, and recommendations based on information gathered by the committee and the committee's deliberations. Each report has been subjected to a rigorous and independent peer-review process and it represents the position of the National Academies on the statement of task.

Proceedings published by the National Academies of Sciences, Engineering, and Medicine chronicle the presentations and discussions at a workshop, symposium, or other event convened by the National Academies. The statements and opinions contained in proceedings are those of the participants and are not endorsed by other participants, the planning committee, or the National Academies.

Rapid Expert Consultations published by the National Academies of Sciences, Engineering, and Medicine are authored by subject-matter experts on narrowly focused topics that can be supported by a body of evidence. The discussions contained in rapid expert consultations are considered those of the authors and do not contain policy recommendations. Rapid expert consultations are reviewed by the institution before release.

For information about other products and activities of the National Academies, please visit www.nationalacademies.org/about/whatwedo.

REDUCING FINANCIAL BARRIERS PLANNING COMMITTEE

GILDA A. BARABINO (*Co-chair*) (NAE/NAM), Olin College of Engineering
THEODORE J. CORBIN, Jr. (*Co-chair*), Drexel University College of Medicine
GEORGE Q. DALEY (NAM), Harvard Medical School
MARC NIVET, University of Texas Southwestern Medical Center
LOUIS W. SULLIVAN (NAM), The Sullivan Alliance to Transform the Health Professions

Project Staff

MARIA LUND DAHLBERG, Senior Program Officer, Roundtable on Black Men and Black Women in Science, Engineering, and Medicine
LYNNETTE LUSENAKA, Program Officer, Roundtable on Black Men and Black Women in Science, Engineering, and Medicine
REGINALD HAYES, Associate Program Officer, Roundtable on Black Men and Black Women in Science, Engineering, and Medicine
MARQUITA WHITING, Senior Program Assistant, Roundtable on Black Men and Black Women in Science, Engineering, and Medicine
TOM ARRISON, Program Director, Policy and Global Affairs (until May 2021)
PAULA W. WHITACRE, Consultant Writer

ROUNDTABLE ON BLACK MEN AND BLACK WOMEN IN SCIENCE, ENGINEERING, AND MEDICINE

ORLANDO KIRTON (Ex Officio Member), Society of Black Academic Surgeons
JOHN R. LUMPKIN (NAM) (Ex Officio Member), Blue Cross and Blue Shield of North Carolina Foundation
SHIRLEY MALCOM (NAS) (Ex Officio Member), American Association for the Advancement of Science
ALFRED MAYS (Ex Officio Member), Burroughs Wellcome Fund
LAMONT R. TERRELL (Ex Officio Member), GlaxoSmithKline

Project Staff

MARIA LUND DAHLBERG, Senior Program Officer, Roundtable on Black Men and Black Women in Science, Engineering, and Medicine
LYNNETTE LUSENAKA, Program Officer, Roundtable on Black Men and Black Women in Science, Engineering, and Medicine
REGINALD HAYES, Associate Program Officer, Roundtable on Black Men and Black Women in Science, Engineering, and Medicine
MARQUITA WHITING, Senior Program Assistant, Roundtable on Black Men and Black Women in Science, Engineering, and Medicine
TOM ARRISON, Program Director, Policy and Global Affairs (until May 2021)

Preface

It is an honor for me to serve as chair of the National Academies of Sciences, Engineering, and Medicine Roundtable on Black Men and Black Women in Science, Engineering, and Medicine, and serve as the editor of this first series of proceedings publications from the Roundtable. Our work originated in 2015 when I and leaders of the W. Montague Cobb/National Medical Association Health Institute recognized the growing absence of Black men in medical schools. In fact, levels of Black men entering medical school reached a historic low in 2015 and 2016. Starting in 2016, and with financial support from important partners such as the Aetna Foundation, the Burroughs Wellcome Fund, the Robert Wood Johnson Foundation, and the Connecticut Legislative Black and Puerto Rican Caucus, we planned a National Academies workshop on issues surrounding the absence of Black men in medicine. The joint workshop entitled "The Growing Absence of Black Men in Medicine and Science" took place in 2017. It was historic, in that to my knowledge it was the first National Academies activity specifically focused on issues involving Black people. The proceedings is entitled *An American Crisis: The Growing Absence of Black Men in Medicine and Science*. It was released in May 2018, and corresponded to a briefing on the subject of Black men and medicine with the Congressional Black Caucus in Washington, D.C. Many of the ideas that emerged from the workshop have been embraced by academia, industry, and philanthropy. But those conversations also highlighted that more needs to be done.

Our next steps have involved the development of a more permanent presence in the National Academies to discuss issues surrounding Black men and

Black women in science, engineering, and medicine. With support from our anchor partners named above, along with the Johnson & Johnson Company, the W. K. Kellogg Foundation, and the University of Pittsburg, and with the continued leadership and commitment from Dr. Victor Dzau, the president of the National Academy of Medicine, the Roundtable on Black Men and Black Women in Science, Engineering, and Medicine was launched late in 2018. I am grateful to the steering committee members for the Roundtable: Drs. L. D. Britt, Cedric M. Bright, George Q. Daley, Randall C. Morgan Jr., Elizabeth O. Ofili, Vivian W. Pinn, and Louis W. Sullivan.

In April 2021, the Roundtable organized a workshop aimed at addressing financial barriers for Black students in science, engineering, and medicine. Financial pressures can create incredible barriers for successfully pursuing scientific careers, and often result in make-or-break decisions regarding students' futures. The overall goal of the workshop was to explore innovative ideas that could ultimately become policies to help ensure the success and vitality of Black students pursuing careers in science, engineering, and medicine.

I am grateful to the co-chairs of the workshop, Dr. Gilda Barabino and Dr. Theodore Corbin Jr. They worked hard to put in place successfully an innovative workshop and create new ideas and new information on the issue of Black students and financing. Reducing financial barriers could appear to be a daunting challenge. As discussed in the proceedings, Black people have historically been placed at a lower point on the economic scale, but current generations have experienced a disturbing downward trend in economic mobility. This, coupled with the rising costs of education, creates an environment that places high financial pressures on Black students interested in science. Participants discussed current strategies ranging from ensconcing students at an early age in science programs, building resilience, and disarming opposition. Some of the most interesting discussions centered on creating systemic changes that would bring about lasting solutions to issues regarding financing. The thoughts and ideas presented in this proceedings are robust, and I believe they provide a blueprint for further action. As with the Roundtable's previous proceedings, they are meant to move us to action. I look forward to viewing the important follow-on work of this action group of the Roundtable.

Cato T. Laurencin, M.D., Ph.D. (NAS/NAE/NAM)
Chair, Roundtable on Black Men and Black Women in Science, Engineering, and Medicine
University Professor, University of Connecticut

Acknowledgments

This Proceedings of a Workshop was prepared by the workshop rapporteurs as a factual summary of what was presented and discussed at the workshop. The planning committee's role was limited to planning and convening the workshop. The statements made are those of the rapporteurs and do not necessarily represent positions of the workshop participants as a whole, the planning committee, or the National Academies of Sciences, Engineering, and Medicine. We wish to extend sincere thanks to all the members of the planning committee for their contributions in scoping, developing, and carrying out this project.

This proceedings has been reviewed in draft form by individuals chosen for their diverse perspectives and technical expertise, in accordance with procedures approved by the National Academies of Sciences, Engineering, and Medicine's Report Review Committee. The purpose of this independent review is to provide candid and critical comments to assist the institution in making its published proceedings as sound as possible and ensure the document meets institutional standards for quality and objectivity. The review comments and draft manuscript remain confidential to protect the integrity of the process. We wish to thank the following individuals for their review of this proceedings: Portia Flowers, National Science Foundation; Misty Heggeness, U.S. Census Bureau; John Rich, Drexel University; Darla Thompson, American Association for the Advancement of Science; and Rochelle Williams, National Society of Black Engineers. Although the reviewers listed above have provided many constructive comments and suggestions, they were not asked to endorse the content of the proceedings, nor did they see the final draft before its release. The review of this proceedings was overseen by Cora Marrett, University of Wisconsin-Madison (retired). Appointed by the National Academies, she was responsible for making certain that an independent examination of this proceedings was carried out in accordance with institutional procedures and that all review comments were carefully considered. Responsibility for the final content of this proceedings rests entirely with the rapporteurs and the institution.

Contents

1

Introduction

The number of Black students in science, engineering, and medicine in the United States has remained disproportionately low over the past several decades. A number of reasons have been identified as contributing to these low numbers, including those related to finances. Financial considerations range from the most immediate—the ability of students to pay for their education and associated costs—to more structural concerns, such as inequities that created and have perpetuated a wealth gap between races and ethnic groups.

The Roundtable on Black Men and Black Women in Science, Engineering, and Medicine of the National Academies of Sciences, Engineering, and Medicine has looked at a range of barriers and solutions related to increasing the nation's number of Black scientists, engineers, and physicians. Previous workshops have been held on such topics as the impact of racism bias (NASEM, 2020), COVID-19 (NASEM, 2021), educational pathways (NASEM, 2022a), and mentoring and advising (NASEM, 2022b). On April 19 and 20, 2021, the Roundtable organized a virtual public workshop to examine financial barriers for Black students in science, engineering, and medicine (SEM), explore existing educational programs to support Black students in SEM, and engage stakeholders in conversations about partnerships and policies that span academia, industry, and philanthropy. With a focus on the data and information available from medical education, presenters throughout the workshop discussed the Black-white wealth gap, opportunities to eliminate debt burden, and specific interventions intended to change the diversity of the workforce. While rich discussions were held during the 2-day workshop, several topics remain for the Roundtable to explore further.

OPENING REMARKS

Welcome from the National Academies Leadership

Victor Dzau, M.D. (Duke University and president of the National Academy of Medicine) represented the National Academies leadership to welcome workshop participants. He thanked the Roundtable for its leadership in exploring and addressing the barriers and opportunities encountered by Black students in pursuing careers in science, engineering, and medicine. He also expressed strong support and commitment on the part of the National Academies for the Roundtable because the low participation rate of African American men and women in SEM threatens the well-being of society and hampers health for the entire population.

Background on the Roundtable

Roundtable chair Cato Laurencin, M.D., Ph.D. (University of Connecticut) thanked Dr. Dzau and the National Academies staff for their support of the Roundtable.

To provide a brief background of the Roundtable, Dr. Laurencin explained it grew out of concern about the lack of Black men entering medicine over the course of several years; some schools reported no Black men in their entering classes. A 2017 workshop resulted in the report *An American Crisis: The Growing Absence of Black Men in Medicine and Science* (NASEM, 2018). This publication generated significant attention, including by members of the Congressional Black Caucus, about the issues underlying this dearth of representation. In 2019, the Roundtable was formed, as Dr. Laurencin explained, "to understand issues impacting Black men and Black women, and to generate ideas for solutions, especially solutions utilizing the strengths in having Black men and Black women in science, engineering, and medicine."

At its December 2019 inaugural meeting, the Roundtable decided to focus on data gathering and ideas generation at each subsequent meeting. Action groups were formed around Racism and Bias, Public Engagement, Mentorship and Advising, Psychological Factors, PreK to Graduate Edu-

BOX 1-1
Workshop Statement of Task

A planning committee of the National Academies of Sciences, Engineering, and Medicine will organize a virtual public workshop to examine the financial barriers—including educational debt burden—preventing Black people from entering or continuing education in science, engineering, and medicine (SEM). The workshop will also identify policies and practices that perpetuate those barriers and lay a foundation of knowledge for others to be better positioned to engage on these issues. Major objectives of the workshop include

1. Identify the existing data and data that are needed to examine trends in financial barriers to Black people pursuing education and careers in SEM;
2. Explore existing educational finance programs and data to support improvements to the effectiveness of those policies and programs; and
3. Cultivate and engage stakeholders in improving the efficacy of educational debt programs through increased investments and partnerships between academia, industry, and government.

cation, and Financing. Each group has held or is planning a workshop, beginning with the workshop on the impact of racism and bias in pursuing careers in science, engineering, and medicine referred to above (NASEM, 2020).[1]

The Public Engagement and Financing action groups collaborated to organize the current workshop, Dr. Laurencin explained. Its purpose is to lead to a better understanding of the financial barriers facing Black students, make a business case related to addressing these barriers, discuss how public and private entities can work together to facilitate students' entry and retention, and reduce overall costs or provide financial support (see Box 1-1 for the workshop Statement of Task).

[1] For more background on the Roundtable, see https://www.nationalacademies.org/our-work/roundtable-on-black-men-and-black-women-in-science-engineering-and-medicine.

Context of the Workshop

Speaking on behalf of the two Roundtable action groups, planning committee co-chair George Q. Daley, M.D., Ph.D. (Harvard Medical School), stated, "The goal for us is to understand the root causes [of financial barriers] but also fundamentally lay a foundation for public engagement and activism by policy makers so as they do not just engage in these issues but also resolve them." He stressed,

> Ultimately, it's our goal to influence the development of policies that build and sustain the workforce of Black engineers, scientists, and physicians for the greater good of our society, which we all know needs to heal, needs to grow, and needs to thrive.

Co-chair Louis Sullivan, M.D. (Sullivan Alliance), added his appreciation to the National Academies for supporting the workshop and to colleagues for working to change the status quo.

ORGANIZATION OF THIS PROCEEDINGS

The remainder of this publication is organized to follow the agenda of the workshop (see Appendix A). Chapter 2 highlights the current situation, with an emphasis on data behind disparate opportunities between Black and white children compiled and analyzed by Opportunity Insights at Harvard University. Chapter 3 reports on previous and current programs, with a focus on those in the health professions and within the federal government. Chapter 4 suggests opportunities envisioned by leaders in physics, medical education, and the private sector. Chapters 5 and 6 report on innovative programs in the philanthropic sector and within academic institutions. Chapter 7 summarizes a brief presentation by Rep. Eddie Bernice Johnson (TX-30) and a "fireside chat" between planning committee co-chair Gilda Barabino, Ph.D. (Olin College of Engineering), and Michelle McMurray-Heath, M.D., Ph.D. (Biotechnology Innovation Organization). The workshop agenda and biographical sketches of the speakers can be found in Appendixes A and B, respectively.

In accordance with the policies of the National Academies, workshop participants did not attempt to establish any conclusions or recommendations about needs and future directions, focusing instead on issues discussed by the speakers and workshop participants. In addition, the planning committee's role was limited to planning the workshop. This proceedings was prepared by rapporteurs as a factual summary of what occurred at the workshop.

REFERENCES

NASEM (National Academies of Sciences, Engineering, and Medicine). 2018. *An American Crisis: The Growing Absence of Black Men in Medicine and Science: Proceedings of a Joint Workshop*. Washington, DC: The National Academies Press. https://www.nap.edu/catalog/25130/an-american-crisis-the-growing-absence-of-black-men-in.

NASEM. 2020. *The Impacts of Racism and Bias on Black People Pursuing Careers in Science, Engineering, and Medicine: Proceedings of a Workshop*. Washington, DC: The National Academies Press. https://www.nap.edu/catalog/25849/the-impacts-of-racism-and-bias-on-black-people-pursuing-careers-in-science-engineering-and-medicine.

NASEM. 2021. *COVID-19 and the Present and Future of Black Communities: The Role of Black Physicians, Engineers, and Scientists: Proceedings of a Workshop*. Washington, DC: The National Academies Press. https://nap.nationalacademies.org/catalog/26146/covid-19-and-the-present-and-future-of-black-communities-the-role-of-black-physicians-engineers-and-scientists.

NASEM. 2022a. *Educational Pathways for Black Students in Science, Engineering, and Medicine: Exploring Barriers and Possible Interventions: Proceedings of a Workshop*. Washington, DC: The National Academies Press. https://nap.nationalacademies.org/catalog/26391/educational-pathways-for-black-students-in-science-engineering-and-medicine.

NASEM. 2022b. *Mentoring of Black Graduate and Medical Students, Postdoctoral Scholars, and Early-Career Faculty in Science, Engineering, and Medicine: Proceedings of a Workshop*. Washington, DC: The National Academies Press. https://nap.nationalacademies.org/catalog/26462/mentoring-of-black-graduate-and-medical-students-postdoctoral-scholars-and-early-career-faculty-in-science-engineering-and-medicine.

2

Addressing Barriers and Opportunities for the Workforce of the Future

Highlights from the Presentations

- A map of the "geography of upward mobility" shows disparities across and within regions, with Black men having the least likelihood of upward mobility compared with white men growing up in families with similar incomes (Dr. Chetty).
- Downward mobility of Black men born into higher-income families is also a concern that cannot be ignored if interventions are to succeed across time (Dr. Chetty).
- Exposure to higher-opportunity environments, at as young an age as possible, increases upward mobility (Dr. Chetty).
- High family income, not just quantitative aptitude, influences the likelihood that a person holds a patent, which serves as a rough proxy for participation in science, engineering, and medicine careers (Dr. Chetty).
- Three areas where research can inform policy to improve mobility relate to (1) reducing segregation, (2) supporting place-based interventions, and (3) improving mobility outcomes at institutions of higher education (Dr. Chetty).
- The number of Black medical students rose from 200 in the 1950s to about 1,600–1,700 today, but that number—only 7 to 8 percent of all medical students—is not on par with

representation of Black people in the overall population (Dr. Sullivan).
- There is an increasing number of Black medical students who identify as women and a decreasing number of Black medical students who identify as men (Dr. Sullivan).

George Q. Daley, M.D., Ph.D., served as moderator for the first panel featuring a data-driven analysis by Raj Chetty, Ph.D. (Harvard University), that served as a point of reference throughout the workshop. In addition, Louis Sullivan, M.D. (Sullivan Alliance), shared a historical perspective about Black representation in medical school and the medical workforce based in part on his decades of experience as a policy advocate, administrative leader, and physician.

NEW INSIGHTS FROM BIG DATA

Dr. Chetty explained he and his colleagues in Harvard University's Opportunity Insights combine "big data" from multiple sources to provide insights on issues related to opportunity and mobility in America. Before homing in on Black Americans in science, engineering, and medicine (SEM), he underscored that while the "American dream is a multifaceted, complicated concept," it can be distilled to one statistic that the data can systematically measure: the percentage of children who grow up to earn more than their parents did.

In a 2017 paper, Dr. Chetty and his colleagues tried to assess how America is living up to the American dream, as measured through upward mobility. They compared children's incomes in their mid-30s with their parents' incomes at around the same age, adjusting for inflation. Almost all children born in 1940 (92 percent) went on to earn more than their parents. However, only about 50 percent of children born in the 1980s have gone on to earn more than their parents. "This is a dramatic trend of interest to economists, as it is a fundamental change in the U.S. economy," Dr. Chetty said. "It is also of interest in a social and political perspective because this trend underlies a lot of the frustration that people around the United States are expressing, including from underrepresented minorities who bear these challenges to a particularly acute degree."

A correlated dimension looks at life expectancy (LE), Dr. Chetty explained, and shows a tight link between LE and income. Men in the bottom 1 percent of income have an average LE of 72 years, versus an average LE of 87 years among men in the top 1 percent, a gap of 15 years. The difference in LE among low- and high-income women is about 10 years.

Fundamental changes in rates of upward mobility are associated with economic, health, social, political, and other outcomes, Dr. Chetty stated. Opportunity Insights also studies how to increase mobility by analyzing a broad range of interventions from childhood to adulthood, using what is referred to as a life-course perspective. The data reveal significant variations. "The starting point for a lot of our work is that the national picture masks very sharp heterogeneity and sharp local differences within America in rates of upward mobility and economic opportunity," he said.

Variations in Mobility

Dr. Chetty shared a map of the country to show "the geography of upward mobility in the United States" (Chetty et al., 2018). He explained the map charts people's life trajectories based on where they were born by combining data on 20 million children born in the early 1980s with anonymized data linking them to their parents' tax returns. It divides the country into 740 urban and rural areas and computes a measure of upward mobility for the children who grew up in each area. Average income at age 35 is derived for children who grew up in low-income families (families who earned about $27,000 or less). There is a tremendous amount of variability, Dr. Chetty pointed out (see Figure 2-1). In some areas, children grow up to have higher levels of income across generations, while in others, the level is stagnant or lower. Parts of the Midwest show high rates of upward mobility from one generation to the next, while much of the Southeast shows lower rates of mobility, for example.

Dr. Chetty acknowledged that some patterns are surprising, using Charlotte, North Carolina, as an example. While Charlotte is considered a rapidly growing area, the children in the study had low mobility and lower earnings compared with their parents. According to Dr. Chetty, "What is happening is that Charlotte is importing talent—lots of people move to Charlotte for high-paying jobs—but low- and middle-income kids growing up in Charlotte, many of them African American, are not necessarily benefiting from that economic growth." He added,

> An area that grows overall does not necessarily lift all boats. That's clear from that example [Charlotte, North Carolina] and, more

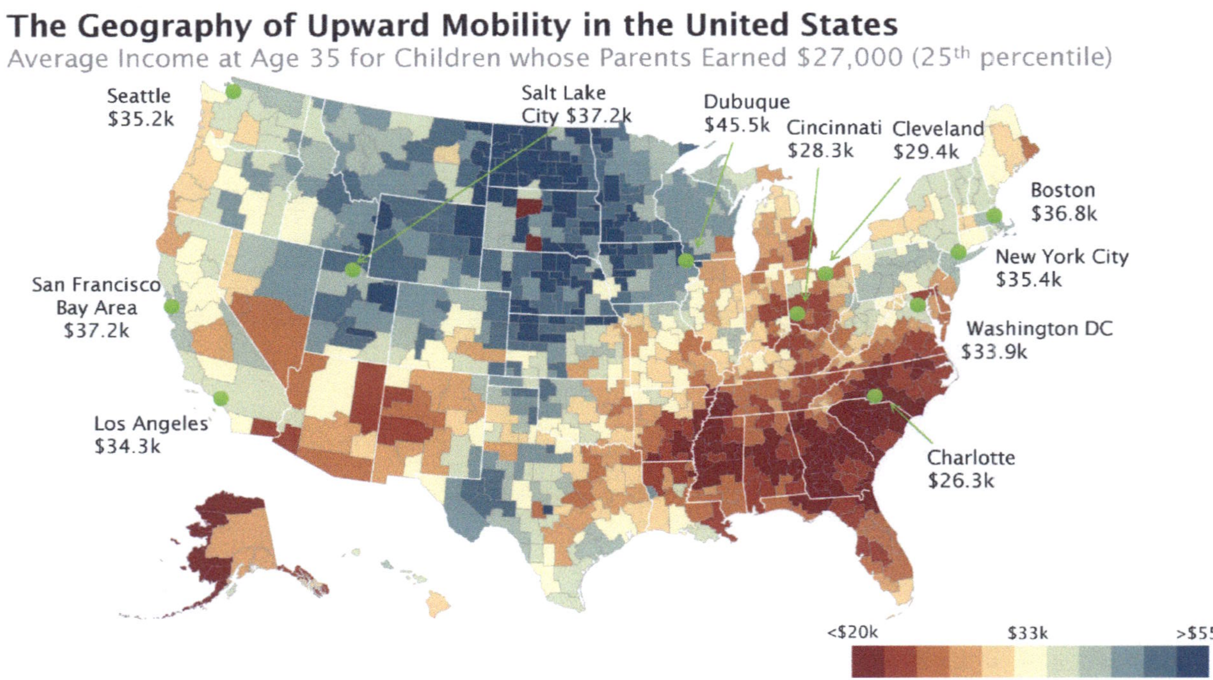

FIGURE 2-1 The geography of upward mobility in the United States.
NOTE: Blue areas indicate more upward mobility; red areas indicate less upward mobility.
SOURCE: Raj Chetty, Workshop Presentation, April 19, 2021, from Chetty et al., 2018.

> generally, looking at data across the U.S. What drives the variation and what are the drivers of economic mobility in the U.S.? I want to focus on the role that racial disparities play. For anyone familiar with the demography of the United States, you might recognize the potential connection between the variations on the map and racial demographics. The areas of the U.S. that have the largest African American populations tend to be the places that have the lowest levels of mobility. Part of what is seen as spatial variation could well be racial variation.

To understand this question further, Dr. Chetty described a subsequent study that linked data from tax returns with U.S. Census data, which allowed the researchers to draw separate maps for Black men and white men (see Figure 2-2) using the same measures as above. "What you are seeing is the power of race in America," Dr. Chetty stated. "It is almost like there are two different countries, one for Black men and one for white men, with nonoverlapping distributions in terms of rates of upward mobility." Expressed differently, the very best places for Blacks in terms of upward mobility have lower mobility than the worst places for white men. "There is no understating the importance of race, even conditional, on class," Dr. Chetty stated.

The data show similar rates of mobility for Black and white women who start out in families at the same income. "There is an intersectionality between race and gender," with the disparities related to upward mobility particularly extreme for men, Dr. Chetty concluded.

In addition to upward mobility, Dr. Chetty said, "the converse channel of downward mobility is also important." He and his team compiled data about income mobility for Black and white men raised in high-income families (those in the top fifth, or quintile, of income distribution). The aim was to see whether the children remain in this top fifth as adults. He characterized a "disheartening pattern" in which most whites remained in the top fifth of income, but Blacks showed more of a cascade downward into lower-income groups. This pattern illustrates a fundamental difference in economic trajectories between Black and white Americans, he said. He continued:

> For white Americans, trying to achieve the American dream is like climbing a ladder from one generation to the next, but for Black Americans, it is like being on a treadmill. Even after you've

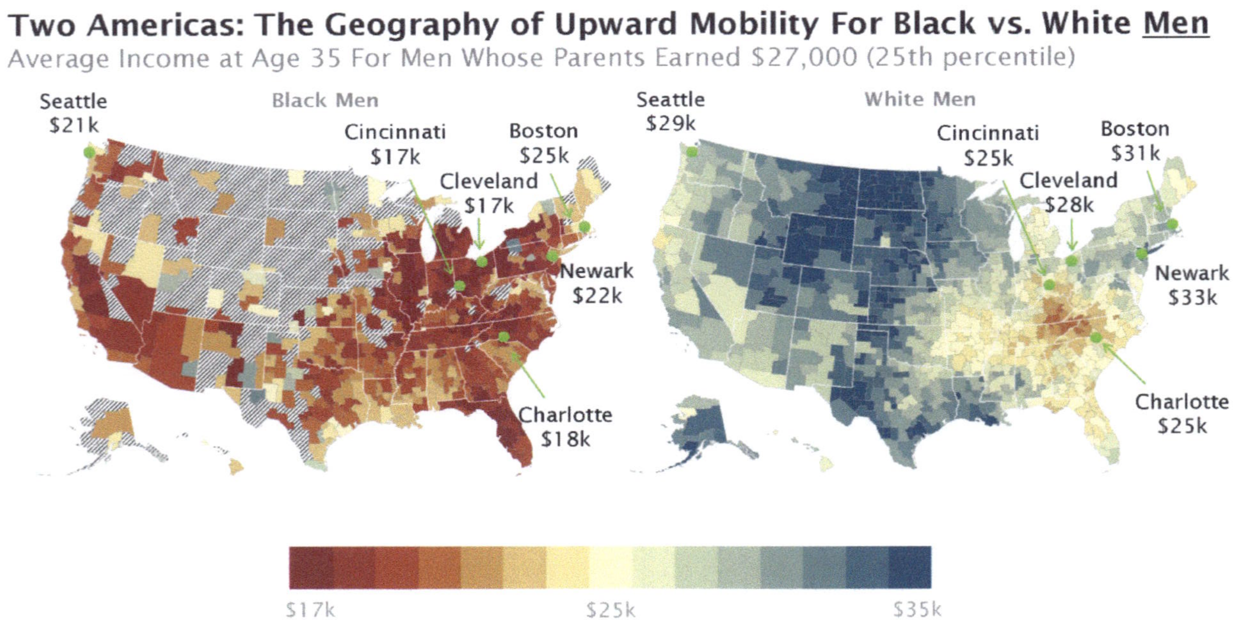

FIGURE 2-2 Two Americas: The geography of upward mobility for Black versus white men.
NOTE: Blue areas indicate more upward mobility; red areas indicate less upward mobility.
SOURCE: Raj Chetty, Workshop Presentation, April 19, 2021, from Chetty et al., 2018.

> climbed up after a generation, there are tremendous structural forces that are pushing [Black men] down that make it necessary to have to make the climb again in the next generation. If we do not fundamentally fix the treadmill phenomenon, no matter what is done to help people rise up, it will not stick in the long run. There are strong forces leading to downward mobility in the next generation. This is a very important point to think of from a policy perspective.

Looking Locally

Dr. Chetty acknowledged that in looking at broad national patterns, one's eyes gravitate to big differences across regions. However, difference can also be viewed at a more granular level within cities with the Opportunity Atlas, a free tool developed by his laboratory.[1] Using New York City as an example, he illustrated how data can be viewed by census tract to reveal varying rates of upward mobility. Stark disparities emerge not only across regions or states but also within them. However, he termed this an encouraging result because he said it suggests that potential solutions may be local and perhaps can be replicated.

To elaborate on this point, Dr. Chetty zoomed in on an address in Brooklyn (531 Sutter Avenue) with a large Black population living in Van Dyke, one of the largest public housing projects in the city. The area shows low rates of upward mobility for Black children. In contrast, a nearby neighborhood with a mixed-income housing development called Nehemiah Houses shows more positive results for children. To understand how, what he termed, "very fine differences in environment" can dramatically change life course, the researchers used tax records to study income gain among 6 million children of families who moved into better neighborhoods. In the Brooklyn case, the children of families who moved from Van Dyke to Nehemiah earned more when they were adults; furthermore, the younger the children were when the families moved, the greater their earnings were as adults.

From this example, Dr. Chetty drew three key lessons:

> First, where you grow up really matters. If you take a given child and move that child from one place to another, you see really

[1] The Opportunity Atlas is available at https://www.opportunityatlas.org/.

> dramatic differences in that child's life outcomes. Second, what seems critical is childhood environment rather than where you are as an adult. Third, there is a "dosage effect" so that for every extra year you are exposed to a better environment, the better your outcomes as an adult.

He and colleagues are now trying to answer what in a different environment helps people thrive. He stressed that none of the factors identified are necessarily causal effects, but are instead correlative and predictive. They include less concentrated poverty, more stable family structures, better school quality, and places with greater social capital and sense of community connectedness. In looking at neighborhoods that have the smallest disparities between Black and white men, a salient set of factors includes low poverty rates among the Black adults in the neighborhood, low levels of racial bias (explicit and implicit), and high rates of the presence of fathers (Chetty et al., 2018). Dr. Chetty noted the "phenomenon of missing Black men in the United States" created by high rates of incarceration and mortality has meant many children growing up in a family without a father. However, Dr. Chetty noted that there appears to be a correlation between fathers being present at the community level and higher rates of upward mobility, possibly related to mentorship, role models, or other reasons.

Disparities in Science, Engineering, and Medicine

Dr. Chetty discussed the implications of mobility research to understand African American underrepresentation in science, engineering, and medicine. He and colleagues focused on scientific innovation and economic growth and, specifically, the lives of 750,000 U.S. patent holders by linking patent records to tax data.

People who become inventors—which he characterized as a rough proxy for SEM achievement—are 10 times more likely to hold a patent if they are born to parents in the top 1 percent of income distribution than to parents with a median income or below. This may be related to childhood environment and quality, but he realized that another reason may relate to families' quantitative aptitudes. Thus, to look at quantitative aptitude, patent rates were plotted against third-grade math test scores. Children in high-income families who scored at the top of their class in third-grade math were much more likely to become inventors than their low- and middle-income counterparts who had similarly high third-grade math scores. In other words, "in America, you need two things to become an inventor or a scientist—high level of quantitative aptitude and being from a rich family," Dr. Chetty said. A similar pattern related to race and ethnicity can be seen, he added, in that Black and Hispanic children who perform as well as white and Asian children in third-grade math are dramatically less likely to go into science and innovation careers as adults. "This leads to an enormous loss of talent in the pipeline that affects society going forward," he said.

He also commented on the importance of exposure to opportunities. Children who grow up in "innovation hubs" such as Silicon Valley in Northern California or Austin, Texas, are more likely to engage in similar types of innovative activities. Patterns are also gender specific. If girls grow up seeing a lot of women in certain innovation fields, they are more likely to become inventors in those fields. "All that evidence suggests that what is going on is that a big part of the reason that Blacks kids are not going into [SEM] careers is they do not have exposure to them," he said. "They are not around a lot of people who have these careers to begin with, which limits their connections, know-how, support, and the like. This has emerged as a key driving force in many studies."

Beyond concerns about justice and equity, diversity in science matters for the nation's strength and gross domestic product, Dr. Chetty said. Referring to "lost Einsteins," his team's work posits that if women, minorities, and children from low-income families invented at the same rate as high-income white men, the innovation rate in America would quadruple (Bell et al., 2019). In addition to an increased quantity of inventors and their inventions, more diversity would change the nature of innovations and improve downstream outcomes, he added.

Diversity also makes a difference in people's health. He referred to an experiment by Alsan et al. (2019) that looked at how doctors' race can affect patient outcomes. The researchers recruited 1,300 Black men in similar health in Oakland, California, and randomly assigned them to Black and white doctors. The patients were told about preventive services (such as diabetes and cholesterol screening) before and after seeing their doctor. After they saw their doctors, the patients assigned to Black doctors were more likely to elect to have the procedures. This is an illustration of the effect of downstream outcomes when there are more Black physicians, Dr. Chetty observed.

Research-Informed Policy Implications

Dr. Chetty concluded by describing how his group conducts research for policy makers. It is organized into three pillars: (1) reducing segregation by helping low-income families move to higher-income areas; (2) place-based investments to increase upward mobility in low-opportunity areas; and (3) improving higher education to amplify the impact of colleges on upward policy.

Related to the first pillar, a recent pilot study in Seattle, Washington, sought to help people move to higher-opportunity areas. The team's mapping showed that people who receive federal housing vouchers tend to cluster in low-opportunity areas and not move to higher-opportunity areas. Working with local housing authorities, they tested if people do not want to move or if elements such as difficulties in the housing search or excessive paperwork create barriers. A randomly selected subset of families with vouchers received additional support to find housing in higher-opportunity neighborhoods, such as customized search assistance, increased landlord engagement, and short-term financial assistance. In the control group, 14.3 percent moved to a higher-opportunity area. In the treatment group, 54.3 percent moved. This small tweak, which added a 2 percent incremental cost to the program, greatly amplified the impact, Dr. Chetty noted. On average, each child who grows up in the higher-opportunity neighborhoods will earn an additional $200,000 over their lifetime. Dr. Chetty noted the results benefited Black people and people of other races and ethnicities, not just white people. The findings from the pilot have or are being used in several pieces of federal legislation.

Related to the second pillar, Dr. Chetty urged participants to engage in "thinking hard about how to invest in neighborhoods," since not everyone can move. His laboratory is involved in an ongoing project, called the Charlotte Opportunity Initiative, that uses a life-course approach, starting with infancy, to change the pipeline of opportunity.[2]

Finally, related to the third pillar, he said, institutions of higher education can do more to contribute to upward mobility. His group has collected data to understand how well students from lower-income families do in achieving upward mobility (going from the bottom 20 percent to the top 20 percent of the income distribution) after attending college. While elite institutions do well in this metric, only a fraction of students from

[2] For more information, see https://opportunityinsights.org/wp-content/uploads/2020/11/OI-CharlotteReport.pdf.

low-income families attend these schools. Most low-income students attend other colleges, including community colleges, that generally have poorer outcomes related to mobility, although with exceptions. He suggested two approaches: expanding access to elite schools and improving outcomes from community colleges.

He concluded that his research points to limitations in improving science, technology, engineering, and mathematics representation without a broader approach. First, he said, it is critical to improve the pipeline of opportunities starting at birth. Second, it is important to reduce downward mobility of affluent Black Americans. Third, exposure and social supports matter beyond just providing financial incentives.

A HISTORICAL PERSPECTIVE

Dr. Sullivan presented a historical perspective to inform the discussion. From the beginning of the American colonies, an equitable environment for Black people has not existed, including for the health care they received. Health care for the Black community came from within the Black community, he related. The first medical schools, formed in the mid-1700s in Philadelphia and New York, did not admit Black students for a century. In 1868, Howard University opened the first medical school for Black students, and seven others, most notably Meharry Medical College, followed in the late 1800s. Medical schools for both Black and white students at the time were largely proprietary institutions with little structured curriculum and often served more as apprenticeships. In the early 1900s, when the Carnegie Foundation commissioned what became known as the *Flexner Report*[3] Abraham Flexner visited all 153 medical schools and found many of them deficient. His report, which recommended adoption of the model used at Johns Hopkins University, sent a shock wave through the medical education establishment, Dr. Sullivan related. Many schools closed, and there were only 80 in 1925. Among Black medical schools only Howard and Meharry continued to operate. The white establishment deemed them necessary to educate some Black physicians to care for the Black community, out of fear that otherwise, contagious disease would pass from the Black to the white community, Dr. Sullivan related.

---

[3] *Medical Education in the United States and Canada: A Report to the Carnegie Foundation for the Advancement of Teaching*, published in 1910 by the Carnegie Foundation, New York City.

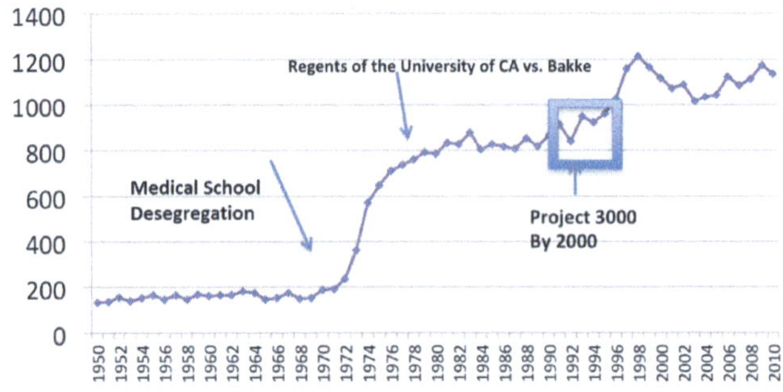

FIGURE 2-3 African Americans graduating from U.S. medical schools, 1950–2010. SOURCES: Louis Sullivan, Workshop Presentation, April 19, 2021, based on *Minority Graduates of U.S. Medical Schools: Trends, 1950–1998*, Washington, DC: AAMC, 2000; and *Diversity in Medical Education Facts and Figures, 2012*, Washington, DC: AAMC, 2012.

The federal government led an expansion in medical education starting in the middle of the 20th century because of a projected shortage of physicians. The number of graduates doubled from 8,000 to 16,000 annually, and 47 medical schools opened in a 25-year period. One-third of the medical schools in the 1950s were in the South; except for the University of Arkansas (which had one Black student), they did not admit Black students. Elsewhere in the country, schools had an occasional one or a few Black students. In the 14 years after the U.S. Supreme Court's *Brown* decision, medical schools in the South had to open up to Black students.[4]

The number of Black medical students increased to 800 in the early 1970s and 1980s, then plateaued (see Figure 2-3). After the assassination of Martin Luther King Jr., universities, including medical schools, made an effort to increase diversity. The Association of American Medical Colleges (AAMC) formed its first committee on Black students in medical schools in 1968, on which Dr. Sullivan served. The committee's bottom line was that medical schools had to be more proactive to integrate and increase the number of Black students. Initiatives increased the percentage of African American students to about 7 to 8 percent of the total medical student population by the end of the century. Now medical schools graduate about 1,600 to 1,700 Black students annually. Of interest, Dr. Sullivan noted, is

[4] *Brown v. Board of Education of Topeka*, 347 U.S. 483 (1954).

the increasing number of Black women and decreasing number of Black men: two out of three Black medical students are women, he reported.

Little progress has been made between the number of Black applicants and matriculants, Dr. Sullivan continued. In 1978, 38 percent of Black men applicants were admitted, and the percentage had not changed 40 years later, in 2018. About 4.5 percent of medical school faculty are Black, and they are less probable to receive National Institutes of Health (NIH) research funding than white applicants (Ginther et al., 2011). Although NIH has initiated a mentoring program and other efforts to improve success rates of Black investigators, "this shows that in the part of the public health system that is supposed to be objective and is allegedly free of bias, this is not the case," Dr. Sullivan said.

Approaches to improve the number of Black medical students and physicians have included mentoring, counseling, and the existence of role models. "We have the challenge in the coming decades—we have made progress, but the amount of progress we have made is far less than what we had hoped for and expected," Dr. Sullivan concluded. He expressed great interest in Dr. Chetty's studies and especially the granularity that his data can bring to find solutions.

DISCUSSION

Dr. Daley commented that the data presented by Dr. Chetty are fascinating but sobering. He noted that Dr. Sullivan made a key connection when he pointed out the modest increase of Black women in medical school but flat or decreasing numbers of Black men, and he connected that trend with Dr. Chetty's data about the mobility gap for Black men. "Understanding that and its root causes is absolutely essential. It's hard not to imagine that structural racism is playing a major factor," Dr. Daley said. The reasons behind the differences might provide important insights, a participant suggested. Dr. Chetty said the answer is not fully known, but it might include issues related to the criminal justice system. Data show in some neighborhoods, upward of 50 percent of Black men are incarcerated on any specific day. Contact with the criminal justice system limits economic and other opportunities going forward. He pointed out that the outcomes of boys of all races are influenced by fathers' presence or, more generally, what the men in their lives are doing. Dr. Chetty added that there is a need to address these factors at a local level and within institutions, not just rely on federal policies changing.

Dr. Sullivan suggested the productivity of Black colleges may be not only because of their academics but also because of role modeling, noting he experienced the effects himself as an undergraduate at Morehouse College. Dr. Chetty agreed that many Historically Black Colleges and Universities (HBCUs) stand out as serving low-income families and have good outcomes. To understand why, he said, one piece of evidence relates to reducing the rates of students who start but do not complete their education. Often, hurdles or shocks (such as a parent losing a job or health problem) derail progress. Targeted support may be inherent in schools with strong social networks such as exist at many HBCUs. It is hard to legislate that approach, he noted. "You have to have people who care about you, people who want to invest in you. That's the message that emerges and the question is how to scale that," Dr. Chetty commented. Dr. Daley also reflected on Dr. Chetty's comments about the importance of early exposure, and he suggested the Roundtable on Black Men and Black Women in Science, Engineering, and Medicine advocate for such programs.

Roundtable member Shirley Malcom, Ph.D. (American Association for the Advancement of Science), commented that some race-attendant policies are experiencing policy and judicial backlash and suggested advocacy and public engagement to make the case that training more Black physicians will lead to better health outcomes. Dr. Sullivan said COVID-19 revealed disparities in the system, and the challenge is to make improved investments permanent.

REFERENCES

Alsan, M., O. Garrick, and G. Graziani. 2019. Does diversity matter for health? Experimental evidence from Oakland. *American Economic Review* 109(12): 4071–4111. DOI: 10.1257/aer.20181446.

Bell, A., R. Chetty, X. Jaravel, N. Petkova, and J. Van Reenen. 2019. Who becomes an inventor in America? The importance of exposure to innovation. *The Quarterly Journal of Economics* 134(2): 647–713. DOI: 10.1093/qje/qjy028.

Chetty, R., J. N. Friedman, N. Hendren, M. R. Jones, and S. R. Porter. 2018. "The Opportunity Atlas: Mapping the Roots of Social Mobility." National Bureau of Economic Research Working Paper 25147. DOI: 10.3386/w25147.

Ginther, D. K., W. T. Schaffer, J. Schnell, B, Masimore, F. Liu, L. L. Haak, and R. Kington. 2011. Race, ethnicity and NIH awards. *Science* 333: 1015–1019.

3

Supportive Workforce Development and Academic Enrichment Programs

Highlights from the Presentations

- Relationships with mentors and advisors are critical to the development of leaders, including of Black physicians (Dr. Satcher).
- Integrated medical schools are important so that all physicians learn to provide effective care to all patients (Dr. Satcher).
- Top challenges identified by student participants in 14 projects funded through the National Workforce Development Pipeline (NWDP) relate to academics and college readiness (28.6 percent), financial barriers (25.7 percent), psychosocial/mental health (20 percent), retention (14.3 percent), and accessibility (11.4 percent) (Ms. Cobb-Souza).
- Common success factors based on 4 years of data show that academic enrichment and early intervention is important in preparing students in reading, math, and science (Ms. Cobb-Souza).
- Early-career exposure, life skills and wellness, and financial support are critical to expose students to role models and career possibilities (Ms. Cobb-Souza).
- High school participants in one summer program—the Pre-Health Career Corps (PHCC) Program—all graduated from high school, and nearly all continued in postsecondary

science, technology, engineering, mathematics, and medicine) (STEMM) pathways, including college, certification programs, or entry-level health employment (Ms. Cobb-Souza).

Planning committee co-chair Theodore Corbin, M.D., M.P.P. (Drexel University), moderated a session to explore solutions to build and invest in Black students pursuing careers in science, engineering, and medicine; promote policies to ensure continued support for these programs; and identify the power and authoritative entities to make change. The presenters were David Satcher, M.D., Ph.D. (Satcher Health Leadership Institute, Morehouse School of Medicine), and Sonsiere Cobb-Souza (Office of Minority Health, U.S. Department of Health and Human Services [HHS]).

THE IMPORTANCE OF RELATIONSHIPS

Dr. Satcher drew from his own experience to discuss the importance and challenges of Black medical students in predominantly white medical schools. Although neither of his parents finished elementary school, he recounted, they were committed to the education of their children. Satcher attended a segregated school 20 miles from his home in Alabama, which he said shaped his and other students' lives. He graduated from Morehouse College in 1963. He related he had some difficulty gaining admission, but he was accepted with the understanding that he maintain a B average and work to pay his tuition. A job in the biology department piqued his interest in research. He also became active in the civil rights movement. When he was seeking to enter medical school, he said, the word was that Duke University would accept one Black student, and many people assumed he would be the student selected. However, he had been jailed several times for his activism, and Duke admitted another Black undergraduate without this history. Although he was initially depressed when he was not accepted, he said looking back, it turned out that "it was one of the best things that happened to me." He was admitted to Case Western Reserve University, where he earned his M.D. and Ph.D.

Dr. Satcher explained that the M.D./Ph.D. program was organized with 1 year of medical school, 2 years in the Ph.D. program, then a return to the medical school. He developed a good relationship with his Ph.D. research advisor, and he had a support system that included financial aid. He also became involved in the community in Cleveland.

He related a pivotal experience in his clinical rotations, which he describes more fully in a recent book (Satcher, 2020). On his first day of an OB/GYN (obstetrics and gynecology) rotation, he was ordered to examine four Black women who were in a room together with no curtains or other privacy between them. He refused because of these conditions, and he walked out. The physician in charge threatened Dr. Satcher's position not only at Case Western but at any institution. The next day, he was called in to see Dean Frederick Robbins. Fearing the worst, Dr. Satcher learned that the other students, all of whom were white, also walked out and that changes would result. This encounter began a relationship with Dr. Robbins that continued until the Nobel laureate's death in 2003. "The point is that the relationship that developed between Fred Robbins and me was a critical part of my own development," Dr. Satcher said. "I've been in a lot of leadership roles. A lot of that occurred because I was fortunate enough to work with people like Fred Robbins, who was an outstanding scholar and who believed in justice." When he spoke at Dr. Robbins's funeral, he recounted how they worked together over the years. He concluded, "I tell this story because I think it's important for everybody, not just the Black students but for all future physicians, that there be a more integrated student body so that students really get to know each other. It helps shape how they approach their patients. Integration of the student body serves a lot of purposes and has made a difference in this country."

HIGHLIGHTS FROM THE NATIONAL WORKFORCE DEVELOPMENT PIPELINE INITIATIVES

Ms. Cobb-Souza provided an overview of the Office of Minority Health (OMH) in the U.S. Department of Health and Human Services. She highlighted past STEMM partnerships, with a focus on the National Workforce Development Pipeline to increase diversity in the health-care pipeline.

Office of Minority Health Partnerships

The mission of OMH is to improve the health of racial and ethnic minority populations through the development of health policies and programs that will eliminate health disparities, Ms. Cobb-Souza explained. OMH has five main functions: promote policy, program, and practice adoption; convene partners; conduct demonstrations and evaluations; disseminate information; and collect and analyze data.

Past STEMM initiatives include the National African American Youth Initiative, Charles R. Drew Graduate Medical Education Program, President and Fellows of Harvard College internship program, and UNCF (United Negro College Fund) Special Programs Corporation. She highlighted the purposes and some of the elements of each program.

National Workforce Development Pipeline

OMH's current STEMM initiative focuses on education, training, and exposure for students. Through the NWDP that began in 2015, 14 projects are aiming to fill the gap in the educational pipeline beginning in middle and high school to increase students' awareness in and pursuit of careers in health care, as well as increase the availability of STEMM programs. The Sullivan Commission (2014) had recommended strengthening K–12 opportunities, she noted, which helped inform the program. About 13 percent of participating students are in middle school, 20 percent are in bridge programs in high school (taking college courses to earn an associate degree), and 67 percent are in high school.

The top challenges identified by students across the projects relate to academics and college readiness (28.6 percent), financial barriers (25.7 percent), psychosocial/mental health (20 percent), retention (14.3 percent), and accessibility (11.4 percent) (see Figure 3-1). Ms. Cobb-Souza noted that the principal investigators in each site had to develop strategies to address these challenges. For example, related to academics and college readiness, many of the students had delays in their reading, math, and science levels, which needed to be addressed. Many students must contribute financially to their households, so some of the programs have provided scholarships or stipends. A significant number were depressed or had other mental or emotional health challenges that called for support services. They need to develop strategies to maintain retention over the 5 to 6 years of the program. Finally, accessibility related to transportation and safety is significant in some locations.

Tools across NWDP programs include summer programming, stipends and scholarships, a wellness life skills curriculum, digital technology and online services, dual enrollment, and internships. She noted that

> common success factors across the 14 programs, based on 4 years of data, show that academic enrichment is vital, as are early-career exposure, life skills and wellness, and financial support.

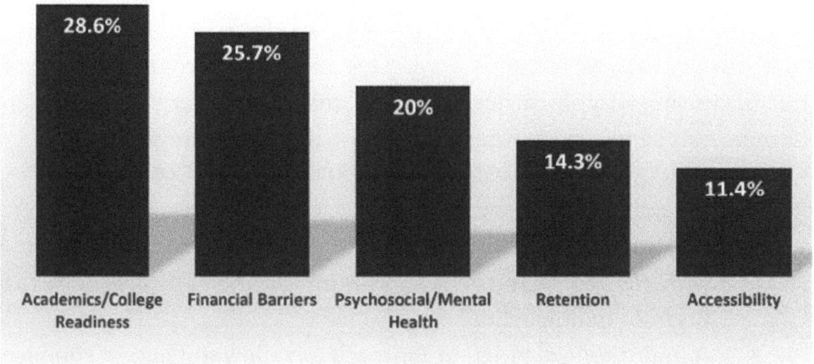

FIGURE 3-1 Top challenges identified by student participants in NWDP programs.
SOURCE: Sonsiere Cobb-Souza, Workshop Presentation, April 19, 2021.

She suggested that lessons learned from NWDP programs can be applied in other settings. As examples, she focused on programs at the University of Hawaii, the Public Health Institute in Oakland, California, and Medgar Evers College in New York City.

The University of Hawaii John A. Burns School of Medicine launched the Pre-Health Career Corps Program. It provides 4 years of summer programming, shadowing, mentoring, and research for high school students. Online learning connects remote students. After 2016, almost 72 percent of students went on to college after utilizing PHCC resources.[1]

The Public Health Institute's FACES for the Future Coalition involves a partnership between 11 high schools and universities.[2] The students receive career exposure, academic enrichment, life skills and wellness support, and youth leadership development. Of note, crisis counseling and case management are provided because 80 percent of the participants come from challenging households or have other family issues. All the students graduated from high school, compared with 70 to 85 percent graduation of comparable students not in the program. In addition, 97 percent continued in postsecondary STEMM pathways, including college, certification programs, or entry-level health employment.

[1] For more information, see https://www.ahec.hawaii.edu/phcc/.

[2] For more information, see https://www.phi.org/our-work/programs/faces-for-the-future-coalition/.

The Medgar Evers Health Careers Connection Pipeline is a bridge program in New York City with two cohorts, Ms. Cobb-Souza explained.[3] Students in the last 2 years of high school take classes to earn an associate degree when they leave high school. This allows them to advance to college or nursing school. Participating students have higher passing rates in Regents math and science exams than those not in the program.

From these programs, Ms. Cobb-Souza drew five lessons learned:

- Inspiration in STEMM subjects and careers needs to begin early, with the highest rates of success for the NWDP programs that begin in middle school.
- A multipronged program approach can allow students to complete STEMM and health programs while linking them to associate degree programs or other allied health training.
- Continued funding support ensures sustainability of program success to include individual student stipends, academic preparation, and ongoing state and federal initiatives.
- Culturally and linguistically effective early pipeline programs can train students from backgrounds that are underrepresented in science.
- Strong partnerships and collaboration are needed to ensure a whole student approach. Family engagement is also essential.

Ms. Cobb-Souza concluded with thanks to the 14 programs and their partners.

DISCUSSION

Dr. Corbin noted the presentations by Dr. Satcher and Ms. Cobb-Souza reinforce the importance of a supportive environment early on. When asked about students who do not complete the pipeline programs, Ms. Cobb-Souza said that those who exit can reenter and, in any event, the awardee organizations have committed to additional engagement with these students, such as through their counseling and wellness programs.

Dr. Louis Sullivan (Sullivan Alliance) referred to the data presented by Dr. Raj Chetty (Harvard University; see Chapter 2) about the impact of early interventions on adult earning capacity. He asked Ms. Cobb-Souza if OMH has looked at programs to intervene before middle school, perhaps in cooperation with the Department of Education. "Would we have greater success if we intervened earlier?" he asked. Ms. Cobb-Souza agreed that early intervention helps. Students often enter the programs with lower levels of reading and math proficiency. The programs do not set minimum academic requirements to participate, and some of the greatest successes have been with students who entered the program behind the expected level. These students had the greatest improvement in academic performance at the middle school level. She added that OMH recently funded interventions targeted at grades 1 to 3. Dr. Sullivan urged offering mentorships and other programs at young levels.

Dr. George Daley (Harvard Medical School) asked the presenters about the value of investing in mentorship skills training, rather than hoping that good intentions or happenstance will suffice. Dr. Satcher commented that he was fortunate to have mentors at Morehouse and in his M.D./Ph.D. program, and he agreed with the need to invest in mentorship. Ms. Cobb-Souza said in internship and other initiatives across HHS that bring in students, the agency must commit to providing mentors to guide students. She agreed that mentorship skill training is needed. In answer to another question, Ms. Cobb-Souza said pipeline programs are being reviewed across HHS to improve coordination and minimize duplication.

Dr. Corbin observed that Dr. Satcher discussed the importance of Black students attending predominantly white institutions. Many medical schools have a holistic approach to admissions, Dr. Corbin said, but there are still challenges in admissions. Dr. Satcher reiterated that, to him, an integrated student body in medical school is important for patient relationships because, currently, Black patients do not necessarily do as well with white physicians as with Black physicians. "We want to get to the point where all physicians are prepared to provide the level of service and they are effective in taking care of patients of any race," Dr. Satcher said.

Returning to the subject of early interventions, Dr. Satcher said one of the most important programs at the Satcher Health Leadership Institute is a program for young parents on how their children develop. Even while their babies are in utero, it is important for parents to feel comfortable in their role to help their children in the long run. Dr. Sullivan commented that one of the striking aspects of Dr. Chetty's research (see Chapter 2) was the influence of place when families move to more affluent areas. Not everyone can move, which argues for investing in school systems nationwide so that all students have smaller classes, experienced teachers, and role models. Programs based on Dr. Chetty's research could be developed with HHS, the Department of Education, and state education departments, he suggested.

"Short of that, we are always remediating and making up for deficiencies in the system that occur early on," Dr. Sullivan stated.

Planning committee co-chair Gilda Barabino, Ph.D. (Olin College of Engineering), urged the importance of thinking about context and environment for success, and to consider "successful practices" rather than "best practices." Programs can have the same elements but work differently in different places. Ms. Cobb-Souza agreed and noted that an OMH program evaluation is reviewing current efforts to identify evidence-informed practices.

Dr. Daley suggested an important conclusion from both sessions of the workshop so far is the need to start early and for educators at all levels to be not just good teachers but also mentors to encourage ambitions, recognizing the influence of self-fulfilling prophecies and expectations. Dr. Corbin suggested that mentorship and education be part of the faculty promotion process as part of scholarly activity. At the same time, he acknowledged the "minority tax"—the commitment to mentoring Black students at the expense of one's own research—is real. To change the environment to be more supportive and encouraging while also protecting the time of minority faculty, Dr. Sullivan suggested resources that are not being fully used, including physicians in the community who can serve as mentors and role models.

REFERENCES

Satcher, D. 2020. *My Quest for Health Equity: Notes on Learning While Leading.* Baltimore, MD: Johns Hopkins University Press.

Sullivan Commission. 2014. *Missing Persons: Minorities in the Health Professions.* https://campaignforaction.org/wp-content/uploads/2016/04/SullivanReport-Diversity-in-Healthcare-Workforce1.pdf.

4

Creating Opportunities for the Future

Highlights from the Presentations

- A survey of physics students conducted for the American Institute of Physics (AIP) TEAM-UP report identified a sense of belonging; development of a "physics identity"; academic, personal, and financial support; and leadership as critical to increasing the number of Black students who earn bachelor's degrees in physics and astronomy (AIP, 2020) (Dr. Gates).
- A major recommendation of the TEAM-UP report is creation of a $50 million endowment to relieve student debt burden and support physics departments in increasing the number of Black students who earn bachelor's degrees in physics and astronomy (Dr. Gates).
- Since 1987, for every four matriculants who enter medical school, one comes from the highest 5 percent in terms of household income, one comes from the rest of the fifth quintile (highest 20 percent of income), one comes from the fourth quintile, and one comes from all three lowest quintiles combined (Dr. Young).
- Association of American Medical Colleges (AAMC) data show that about 50 percent of Black medical students attend a private medical school, the highest percentage among races and ethnic-

ities, and Black students graduate with the highest median level of debt (Dr. Young).

- Students must gain financial literacy early so they enter medical school understanding the debt and other obligations they are assuming, as well as federal and other opportunities that may be available to them (Dr. Graham).
- Nontraditional paths, such as in the technology industry, provide a way for Black medical graduates to have a significant effect on their communities in different settings (Dr. Graham).

The workshop continued with a session moderated by Theodore Corbin, M.D., M.P.P. (Drexel University), to examine the opportunities to eliminate students' debt burden while exploring opportunities and contingencies in science, engineering, and medicine for Black students. Sylvester James Gates Jr., Ph.D. (Brown University), described a major effort within the physics community to increase the number of African Americans with bachelor's degrees in physics and astronomy. Geoffrey Young, Ph.D. (Association of American Medical Colleges), shared data about students attending medical school and AAMC resources available to current and future medical students. Garth Graham, M.D., Ph.D. (Google), used his own experience as a student with little familiarity with the financial implications of his decisions, as well as his career, to suggest alternate pathways for Black scientists, engineers, and physicians to make a positive impact.

INITIATIVES IN THE PHYSICS COMMUNITY

Dr. Gates shared that his work as a theoretical physicist leads him to ponder large concepts of space and time, while his identity as an African American physicist provides a perspective on his discipline. To frame his presentation, he shared three "voices from the past." Physicist Albert Einstein said, "Imagination is more important than knowledge. For knowledge is limited to all we now know and understand, while imagination embraces the entire world, and all there will be to know and understand." Computer scientist Alan Turing said, "Sometimes it is the people no one can imagine anything of who do the things no one can imagine." Scholar and Holocaust survivor Elie Wiesel said, "The opposite of love is not hate, it is indifference." To Dr. Gates, these three quotations sum up why diversity is so important in science and engineering and the need to fight against indifference. Dr. Gates noted Einstein's relationships with Black leaders including W. E. B. Dubois, and he referred participants to a book about Einstein's views on race and racism that helps explain why scientists should be involved in issues of diversity, equity, and inclusion (Jerome and Taylor, 2006).

In 2017, the AIP, a consortium of physics organizations, launched an effort that resulted in the report *The Time Is Now: Systemic Changes to Increase African Americans with Bachelor's Degrees in Physics and Astronomy* (AIP, 2020). Dr. Gates was a member of the TEAM-UP task force that developed the report. In discussing the removal of barriers, he said, the task force concluded that finance was at the root of the problem, including systemic issues related to the wealth gap between Blacks and whites. Similar homes in mostly Black neighborhoods are valued 23 percent less than in mostly white neighborhoods, Gates reminded the group. Because schools are primarily funded through local property taxes based on home values, housing discrimination affects school funding, which affects education quality.

The report also surveyed physics students. The survey revealed five factors that students consider to be essential, the absence of which can block the pipeline to earning bachelor's degrees: (1) fostering a sense of belonging for African American student persistence and success; (2) developing a "physics identity," in which African American students must perceive themselves, and be perceived by others, as future physicists and astronomers; (3) effective teaching and a strength-based approach to academic support; (4) support to offset financial burdens and stress; and (5) leadership and structures that prioritize creating environments, policies, and structures that maximize African American student success (AIP, 2020). An important part of the TEAM-UP report, he added, is the need for change management, noting "a new level of thinking is required to solve a persistent problem." While the report is broader than finances, he said he would focus on this factor, given the workshop theme.

In talking to students about finances, key findings surfaced, as Dr. Gates related:

> The enormous racial wealth gap creates financial stresses for Black students. Working on and off campus can impede academic progress and continuation to degree. Mental health stress related to financial stress was also significant. Student retention was found to improve when students were recognized as individuals with unique and intersecting social identities and experiences such as

first-generation college students or working to support a family. It is important for faculty to provide that support.

A graph in the report shows the needs (see Figure 4-1). When asked about concerns about paying for college, 44 percent of African American students strongly agreed they had this concern, compared with 27 percent of white students and 30 percent of Black/mixed-race students.

The report can serve as a handbook for institutions and organizations affiliated with physics that want to make a difference, Dr. Gates noted in highlighting its recommendations (AIP, 2020). For example, departments should identify campus resources for emergency financial aid, conference travel, and other unmet needs that would help African American students to persist in the discipline. Second, faculty should seek funding for undergraduate students to work in research groups or as learning assistants and find other ways to help students academically advance while earning money. Third, faculty and staff should normalize seeking help by discussing stress and self-care with students and referring them to campus resources.

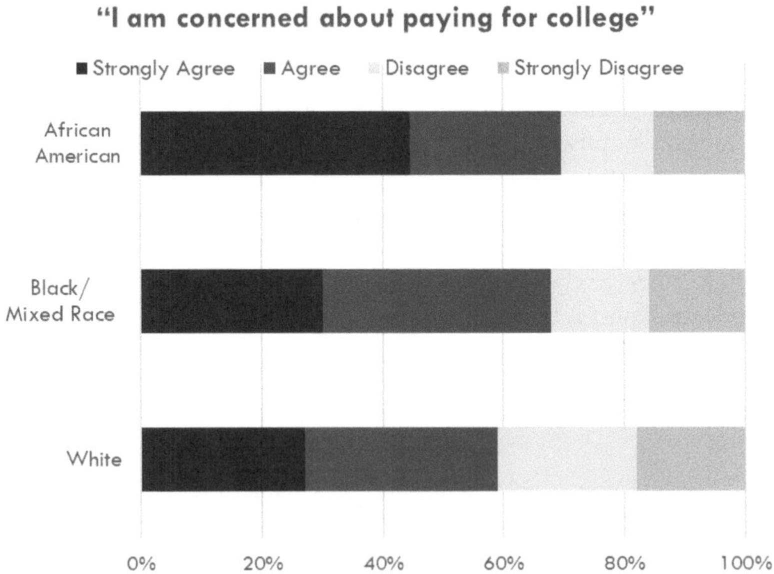

FIGURE 4-1 Students' concerns about paying for college vary by race.
SOURCE: Sylvester James Gates Jr., Workshop Presentation, April 19, 2021. Recreated from AIP, 2020, p. 45.

Finally, what Dr. Gates referred to as the "blockbuster" is the report's recommendation that a consortium of physical science societies should raise a $50 million endowment from foundations and philanthropic sources to support minority students with unmet financial needs in physics and astronomy and to support departments' implementation of the report's other recommendations. As an interim step, physics and astronomy societies should raise $1.2 million per year to relieve the debt burden of African American degree students.

The recommendation of the $50-million endowment constitutes "swinging for the fences," Dr. Gates acknowledged. "We don't know if we will be successful, but we know we won't be successful if we don't try. The bottom line of the report is let's go big." He noted the report was written before the events of 2020, and he is more encouraged about success.

AAMC RESOURCES TO MANAGE THE DEBT BURDEN

Dr. Young shared financial data on family income and debt of medical students and graduates, and he described AAMC resources to help alleviate debt. He also spoke about the recently announced AAMC strategic plan, which includes expanded and enhanced support for underrepresented in medicine (URiM) learners.

Dr. Young drew from U.S. Census data as well as two AAMC student surveys. First, the Matriculating Student Questionnaire (MSQ) is given to first-year medical students and asks, among other items, about household income. Second, the Graduate Student Questionnaire (GSQ) is administered to graduating seniors and asks about student debt levels. Dr. Young pointed out that students can be tracked from the MSQ to the GSQ.

Student Income

Dr. Young explained that the median student debt was about $183,000 in 2015 and about $200,000 in 2020. Adjusted for inflation, the debt level across all graduates has been relatively stable over the past 6 years, while the cost of attendance (for 4 years) has increased from $267,000 to $277,000.

Enrollment in college and medical school is not even across all income levels (see Figure 4-2), Dr. Young pointed out. At the undergraduate level, about 11 percent of students who attend college are from the lowest quintile (i.e., the 20 percent of American households with the lowest incomes), while about 37 percent are from the highest quintile (i.e., the 20 percent of

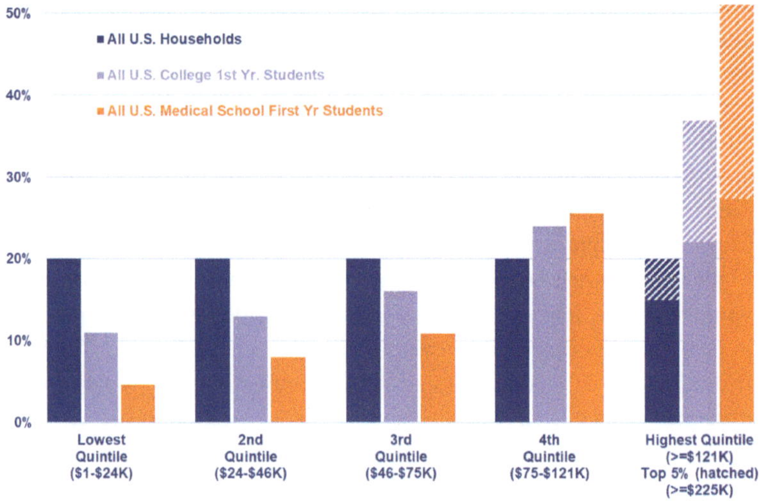

FIGURE 4-2 Percent of first-year U.S. medical students and U.S. college students by household income, 2017.
SOURCES: Geoffrey Young, Workshop Presentation, April 19, 2021, based on U.S. Census data; M. K. Eagan, E. B. Stolzenberg, H. B. Zimmerman, M. C. Aragon, H. Whang Sayson, and C. Rios-Aguilar, 2017, *The American Freshman: National Norms Fall 2016*, Los Angeles: Higher Education Research Institute, UCLA; and Matriculating Student Questionnaire (MSQ), AAMC.

American households with the highest incomes). Wealthier Americans are disproportionately enrolled in U.S. colleges, according to U.S. Census data.

AAMC data represented in Figure 4-2 show that the disparity is even starker in medical school, Dr. Young continued. About 5 percent of first-year medical students come from the lowest quintile, 8 percent from the second-lowest quintile, and 11 percent from the middle quintile. When reaching the fourth quintile, the percentage rises to 26 percent. Fifty percent of medical students come from the highest quintile, with half that number coming from the highest 5 percent by income. "What this is showing is that as your household income increases, you are more likely to attend college and medical school," he said. "The key point is that first-year medical students are not evenly distributed by household income." Expressed another way, Dr. Young said,

> For every four matriculants who enter medical school, one will come from the highest 5 percent, one is going to come from the

rest of the highest quintile, one will come from the fourth quintile, and one will come from the three lowest quintiles combined that represent 60 percent of the U.S. population. These data have been consistent since 1987.

Black Medical Students and Debt

Dr. Young summarized findings from a recent AAMC report on the debt burden among Black medical graduates (AAMC, 2020). Black medical students have the highest level of education debt,[1] are among the highest percentage with scholarships to support their medical education, have the lowest level of medical education financed by "personal/relatives" funds, and have one of the lowest median parental income levels (see Table 4-1).

Dr. Young referred to the study as a "nuanced narrative." For example, the type of medical school affects debt level and varies by race, with 50 percent of Black students attending private medical schools. The higher costs of private schools compared with public schools is one driver of debt levels, Dr. Young said. About 91 percent of Black students graduate with debt, the highest of any group, with a median amount of $230,000 in debt. Very few (about 8 percent) have funds from family members to pay expenses.

Dr. Young next looked at how a doctor's starting salary might affect a case of $230,000 in education debt, looking at family medicine (median starting salary is $200,000), emergency medicine ($250,000), and cardiology ($300,000). He broke out living expenses into four categories: taxes, loan repayments, housing costs, and other living expenses. Dr. Young explained that the REPAYE (Revised Pay As You Earn) federal repayment plan ties repayment to income rather than debt level.[2] With this system, students (including Black and African American students) will be able to repay their education debt, afford their living expenses, and save for retirement, no matter their specialty, barring unique circumstances.

AAMC Resources and Strategic Plan

AAMC data show that the number of students who are URiM, as well as students from low-income families, has remained stagnant over the last

[1] Both medical school debt and premedical, including college, debt.

[2] For information on this program, see https://studentaid.gov/manage-loans/repayment/plans/income-driven.

TABLE 4-1 Education Debt Data for 2019 Medical School Graduates by Race and Ethnicity

Race or Ethnicity	With Education Debt	Median Education Debt of Indebted Graduates	Public/Private School	Reported Scholarship Funds	Median Self-Reported Parental Income	Average for percentage of Medical Education to be financed with:		
						"Personal/Parents/ Relatives/ Spouses/ Partners" Funds	"Scholarship with or without a Service Commitment/Work-Study" funds	Loans
All	73%	$200,000	61/39	62%	$130,000	24%	19%	56%
American Indian and Alaska Native, alone or in combination	80%	$212,375	71/29	84%	$90,000	14%	33%	25%
Asian, not Hispanic	61%	$180,000	56/44	56%	$120,000	33%	17%	49%
Black, not Hispanic	91%	$230,000	50/50	83%	$80,000	8%	34%	57%
Hispanic	84%	$190,000	57/43	65%	$70,000	13%	25%	61%
White, not Hispanic	75%	$200,000	65/35	61%	$150,000	24%	17%	58%
All others, mostly those reporting multiple combinations of race and ethnicity or "other"	71%	$200,000	59/41	64%	$110,000	24%	23%	53%

NOTES: Also available from AAMC report *Physician Education Debt and the Cost to Attend Medical School: 2020 Update*, https://store.aamc.org/physician-education-debt-and-the-cost-to-attend-medical-school-2020-update.html. Education debt is the sum of both medical school debt and premedical, including college, debt.

SOURCE: Reproduced from Geoffrey Young, Workshop Presentation, April 19, 2021, from AAMC Medical School Graduation Questionnaire (GQ), 2019, and the corresponding Matriculating Students Questionnaire (MSQ).

15 years, despite larger medical school populations. At its core, he said, this underrepresentation tracks back to systemic racism, structural inequities, and access to education, housing, health care, food security, and criminal justice. These inequities, coupled with exclusionary admissions processes and institutional culture, further impede an already narrow pathway defined by traditional academic medicine. "I propose we have to start upstream, to try to address the inequities, before learners apply to medical school," he stated.

Dr. Young described a number of AAMC resources. Its Fee Assistance Program provides support for some of the costs associated with medical school applications and examinations. He noted changes in eligibility criteria.[3] He also noted an 18 percent increase in overall applicants in 2021 over 2020, including a 31 percent increase in URiM applicants. Among URiM applicants in 2021, 51 percent identified as Black or African American. Women were 68.5 percent of the African American Fee Assistance applicants and men were 31.5 percent. What will be telling is whether this pool of Fee Assistance applicants reflects who matriculates, he added.

Other AAMC resources include financial information, services, and tools (see Box 4-1).

Through the AAMC Strategic Plan, the association is committed to making a difference by working upstream, according to Dr. Young. The plan has 10 actions, including one that he leads that aims to significantly diversify the medical school applicants and matriculants. Achieving this goal requires addressing systemic barriers, he said. Three pillars to achieve it are to leverage data for change; to widen the path to medicine and the health professions by identifying, supporting, and disseminating effective interventions for learners across the educational continuum (including working with partners in the K–12 space); and to address climate and culture in the transition to medical school.[4]

ALTERNATE CAREER PATHWAYS

Dr. Corbin asked Dr. Graham to talk about his personal experiences and leadership in government and industry. Dr. Graham said he would start

---

[3] For the full eligibility requirements of the AAMC Fee Assistance Program, see https://students-residents.aamc.org/fee-assistance-program/fee-assistance-program.

[4] For more information, see "A Healthier Future for All: The AAMC Strategic Plan" at https://www.aamc.org/what-we-do/strategic-plan/healthier-future-all-aamc-strategic-plan.

BOX 4-1
AAMC Debt Resources for Students and Schools

AAMC provides information, tools, and other resources that can be found on the AAMC website (http://www.aamc.org).

Financial Information

- Financial aid fact sheets
- Debt, Costs, and Loan Repayment Fact Card (for a medical student's education)
- Loan repayment information

Resources

- Education Debt Manager
- Data analysis reports
- AAMC Financial Wellness Program
- Loan Repayment/Forgiveness/Scholarship and Other Programs database
- Loan Repayment Timeline chart

Services

- Customized onsite/webinar school presentations
- Webinars and on-demand videos
- Pre-med outreach and support

Tools

- MedLoans® Organizer and Calculator
- Interactive budgeting worksheets for students and residents

with the context of what Black and Brown communities are facing and the factors that lead to debt burden.

Dr. Graham grew up in Miami where the Robert Wood Johnson Foundation has found a 20-year difference in life expectancy between his community in North Miami compared with more affluent areas in the region. Many Black and Brown medical students, including him, start a life journey that begins with that set of experiences:

> By the time we reach medical school, there are experiences that both drive future decisions but also things from the past that we accumulate and bring to the table, both positives and challenges.

> The conclusion is that without understanding both the intricacies of financing their education, the social dynamics they bring toward financing that education, and potential opportunities for income, we minimize the potential that Black and Brown students can make in a variety of different contexts.

He recalled that by the time he reached medical school, "I did not really understand the debt papers I was signing, I was just thrilled to be there. If the financial aid office put something in front of me, I signed it as a ticket and opportunity to upward mobility." He noted he did not understand the concept of debt burden or of future economic dynamics to pass resources on to future generations.

> My first takeaway point is that issues around debt burden and financing extend beyond the medical school experience into ways that Black and Brown students are educated about financing in general. We should focus efforts, whether through mentorship or formal efforts, to educate Black and Brown students early in the process about the financing of medical school education.

Data around net worth and income of Black physicians show a disparity, and the capacity to continue upward mobility and pass wealth on to children is a challenge (see also Chapter 2). Black men and boys from higher-income Black families still face challenges to get through educational systems and move ahead. "It's important to understand generational dynamics," Dr. Graham said. "We are not necessarily creating wealth even if we make it to medical school."

Debt burden influenced his career decision-making when he graduated medical school and went on to training, he said. When he went to work at the Department of Health and Human Services, he learned about programs he was not aware of as a student, such as the National Institutes of Health (NIH) loan repayment program,[5] Health Resources and Services Administration (HRSA) loan repayment program,[6] and others across the federal government. "My point is two-fold. First, make sure students understand

---

[5] For more information, see the NIH Division of Loan Repayment website at https://www.lrp.nih.gov.

[6] For more information, see the HRSA Loan Repayment Program website at https://nhsc.hrsa.gov/loan-repayment/index.html.

these opportunities early on, and second, continue to support these programs as vital to keep the pipeline open," Dr. Graham said.

He also urged exposing students to nontraditional career paths that allow for mobility. When he left the federal government, he went into academic research, then on to positions in industry. "The tech industry has had a long challenge in recruiting minority professionals from different backgrounds, but the industry has an impact on day-to-day life," said Dr. Graham. "There is an important need to have Black and Brown voices at those tables, especially in leadership positions." These opportunities allow Black and Brown students to contribute to communities through nuanced ways, he said. He wants to "open the eyes of our communities to opportunities, to different pathways from medical and health services training and background, and to succeed and manage finances appropriately." With multiple opportunities for influence and advancement, he urged mentoring students to consider both traditional clinical and nontraditional clinical paths.

He also called for diversifying corporate boards. The lack of Black and Brown members of these major boards is a lost opportunity, he underlined. These companies affect communities' lives. "I never would have thought of that, but now I see that my experiences are essential to those companies," he said. He urged the Roundtable on Black Men and Black Women in Science, Engineering, and Medicine to think of "all the different ways we can inspire, educate, and mentor and push through people with different backgrounds like mine to achieve impact," he stated.

Dr. Graham concluded with three recommendations. First, he called for understanding the context of students from challenging backgrounds and educating them about finances early. Second, he said it is important to understand the impact of federal programs and what they allow students to do. He noted the programs have been under attack and advocacy is necessary. Third, he recommended exposing students to successful nontraditional career paths in high tech and other industries.

DISCUSSION

In answer to a question about whether the TEAM-UP project found different outcomes based on institution type (specifically Historically Black Colleges and Universities [HBCUs] compared with Predominately White Institutions, or PWIs), Dr. Gates said the answer depends on the outcome looked at. If the outcome is completion of undergraduate degree, HBCUs perform better. If the outcome is a long-term career in research, the data get more complicated, he said.[7]

During a discussion about medical school admission rates, Dr. Young said one way to narrow the disparity is for multiple communities to educate and work with admissions officers and committees who serve as the gatekeepers. It is important to emphasize holistic admissions that will enrich the learning environment in line with the mission of the medical school, he noted. Schools make decisions about the type of physicians they want to train. To the point about students' lack of financial literacy, he agreed schools do not always do a good job in explaining what is involved and possible resources. AAMC programs can help, but students should start learning in high school and college about medical school costs. Once students are in school, it is important to think how they will thrive, he added. "I have seen too many students, especially Black men, go to a top medical school and experience difficulty because it is not a good place for them. The social environment affects students' ability to thrive," he said. He stressed the need for support from leadership.

Dr. Louis Sullivan (Sullivan Alliance) asked Dr. Gates about the goal for the AIP-proposed $50 million endowment fund in terms of the number of Black physicists. Dr. Gates noted that from 1999 to 2017, about 5 percent of physics degree recipients were Black, and the goal of an extended effort would be to double the number. Dr. Daley asked about trends in physics degrees. Dr. Gates said the number of Americans getting degrees in physics has roughly doubled in recent years, but the level has stagnated among African Americans. A decrease in the overall number of undergraduate physics degrees in the 1990s led to an earlier AIP report, called SPIN-UP, that was very effective (AIP, 2003). He continued, "I think COVID-19 will give all the STEM (science, technology, engineering, and mathematics) fields a burst. This is a second Sputnik moment."

Related to increasing the number of Black medical students, Dr. Young said AAMC anticipates a physician shortage by the early 2030s. Thirty new medical schools have been opened in the past 20 years, but diversity within those schools has not increased. AAMC is calling for strengthening pipeline programs and mechanisms to identify effective practices. He noted the AAMC strategic plan looks across the continuum of medical education. For example, he said, "Resources are needed to support young learners so they

[7] Further discussion can be found at https://www.aip.org/diversity-initiatives/team-up-task-force or in AIP, 2020.

are ready and prepared to be competitive. Once in school, potential barriers must be addressed. There is a cap on the number of residency programs, and those numbers need to increase. All these efforts must be undertaken in a sustained way with long-term commitments."

Dr. Sullivan observed that in the 1950s and 1960s, members of Congress were often effective in obtaining funding for the medical centers in their districts. More broadly, said Dr. Sullivan, "We have lost faith in ourselves as a nation." He called for bold commitments and leadership, similar to the Marshall Plan after World War II and the Great Society in the 1960s. "The nation does not recognize the benefits from these prior investments. My hope is that COVID-19 will open the eyes of what the medical system can provide and what it should do in the future, but we need the people and systems to make that happen," Dr. Sullivan said. Dr. Gates agreed that a loss of confidence is at the core of many difficulties in the country. On a positive note, he pointed out the business community seems to be more involved than previously. "We have to work in partnership with Corporate America," Dr. Gates said. "There is evidence that business understands we cannot go backwards to have leadership."

Dr. Corbin asked Dr. Graham to weigh in on the opportunities for partnerships with the private sector on diversity, equity, and inclusion initiatives. Dr. Graham said the private sector can play an important role, but support has to be consistent and sustained year over year, not just done to achieve visibility. In addition to funding, businesses can provide ways for youths to get involved. He noted the private sector can also influence public discourse and have political impact.

REFERENCES

AAMC (Association of American Medical Colleges). 2020. *Physician Education Debt and the Cost to Attend Medical School.* https://www.aamc.org/data-reports/students-residents/report/physician-education-debt-and-cost-attend-medical-school.

AIP (American Institute of Physics). 2003. National Task Force on Undergraduate Physics. *Strategic Programs for Innovations in Undergraduate Physics*. College Park, MD: American Association of Physics Teachers.

AIP. 2020. National Task Force to Elevate African American Representation in Undergraduate Physics & Astronomy (TEAM-UP). *The Time Is Now: Systemic Changes to Increase African Americans with Bachelor's Degrees in Physics and Astronomy.* https://www.aip.org/sites/default/files/aipcorp/files/teamup-full-report.pdf.

Jerome, F., and R. Taylor. 2006. *Einstein on Race and Racism*. Piscataway, NJ: Rutgers University Press.

5

Fellowships, Philanthropy, and Industry

Highlights from the Presentations

- The Bloomberg Foundation's support of $100 million to four Black medical schools is the largest philanthropic gift that these schools have received individually or collectively (Ms. Ezediaro).
- It is important not to hesitate to engage in controversial issues that are focused on addressing 400 years of systemic racial issues and continue to impact the intergenerational wealth of black families, communities, and institutions (Ms. Ezediaro).
- Collaborations bring groups with different areas of expertise together to achieve a common outcome (Ms. Lezama).
- Real solutions to the problems of underrepresentation of Blacks in the health-care professions will not be solved by tinkering around the edges. Radical solutions are needed (Dr. Iton).
- Reparations could give rise to opportunities for African Americans to repair the legacy of centuries of racism. Historically Black Colleges and Universities (HBCUs) are a prime target for the investment necessary to bring about the repair (Dr. Iton).
- Black contributions to science, engineering, and medicine have been marginalized over the centuries. It is critical to change the narrative in order to reclaim these achievements (Dr. Iton).

James Hildreth, M.D., Ph.D. (Meharry Medical College), moderated a session to explore the role of industry, foundation, and philanthropic support to advance the goal of greater diversity and inclusion in science, engineering, and medicine. After short presentations by Garnesha Ezediaro, B.A. (Bloomberg Foundation), Michele Lezama, M.B.A. (National Action Council for Minorities in Engineering, Inc.), and Anthony B. Iton, M.D., J.D., M.P.H (California Endowment), most of the session was devoted to discussion among the panel and with participants.

BLOOMBERG FOUNDATION

Ms. Ezediaro focused on the Bloomberg Foundation's partnerships with four historically Black medical schools: Meharry Medical College, Morehouse School of Medicine, Howard University, and Charles R. Drew University of Medicine. The foundation provided $100 million to these schools. "For us, it was alarming that these schools had not received a gift of this size in the past, individually or collectively," she commented. She explained how the foundation decided to partner with the institutions. They started with data on the contribution of Black doctors to health, the debt of Black students entering and leaving medical school, and the long-term upstream impact of medical debt on communities. She explained, "We are not only focused on students but also years down the line, the students who can service communities." The foundation did not approach the schools in a prescriptive way, she said, but asked how a partnership could be most meaningful. The gift provides up to $100,000 in debt relief for students and funding to institutions for wrap-around services.

She noted that scholarships are an important part of philanthropy, but she urged thinking of different models of funding. The excitement for a student to wipe away debt is very impactful, she said. She added the hope is that more foundations will support institutions to build capacity.

NATIONAL ACTION COUNCIL FOR MINORITIES IN ENGINEERING

Ms. Lezama explained that NACME (the National Action Council for Minorities in Engineering) was founded in 1976 to focus on engineering and computer science. Concurring with comments by other speakers, she said NACME has found that the top factors that explain why more Black students do not enter or graduate in these fields include preparation and financial need.

Ms. Lezama agreed with the need expressed by other presenters for corporate involvement and public-private partnerships. NACME keeps executives aware of relevant issues not only to increase their financial contributions to minority students but also to provide them access to competitive opportunities, such as in Silicon Valley. NACME works through partnerships with 40 universities, including four HBCUs. She noted the association is also looking at debt relief scholarship models and advocating for corporations to support them.

CALIFORNIA ENDOWMENT

Dr. Iton explained the mission of the California Endowment is to expand access to affordable, quality health care for underserved individuals and communities and to promote fundamental improvements in the health status of all Californians. Several years ago, Dr. Iton oversaw a health workforce study when it was recognized that implementation of the Affordable Care Act (P.L. 111-148) could provide new workforce pathways for students of color in the state. Through $130 million from the Endowment, efforts to diversify and expand the workforce were supplemented through loan repayments, scholarships, and increased residency spots, especially in low-income and communities of color that are under-doctored. He explained that California's Proposition 209 bans the state from participating in affirmative action, but as a private foundation, the Endowment can earmark dollars.

In recruiting, supporting, and encouraging underrepresented minorities in the health professions, barriers to entry into these professions for African Americans, especially men, were identified. An analysis showed that African American students are affected much earlier in the pathway than at medical school. Many students experience a bottleneck at the community college level. Thus, the Endowment has started to focus earlier along the pipeline, especially on grades 9 to 12 and then into college. A partnership with a group called Health Career Connection has helped tighten the pathway programs, Dr. Iton said. He continued,

> The bottom line is that it seems to me that we need a radical solution. We are not going to solve the problem with tinkering around the edges as we have done for decades. Access to pre-college and pre-medical school science training to equip especially African American males to meaningfully participate in the 21st century economy and health career space is needed.

He suggested a combination of online training and partnerships and that Silicon Valley and HBCUs can help greatly expand access. "We have to dramatically increase the pipeline of students who are prepared. We need something radical, not do the same things we have always done, with incremental increases," he stressed.

DISCUSSION

Picking up from Dr. Iton's observation about a focus on the earlier grades, Dr. Hildreth commented that preparation comes down to the quality of K–12 schools, which is linked to families' incomes. He asked the presenters about solutions and the role of their organizations.

Ms. Lezama said that NACME has set what they call "big hairy audacious goals." The first is a national bridge program. She noted that virtual opportunities can be created to give children, no matter where they live, access to the rigor needed to prepare for careers in engineering and computer science. To increase graduation rates, it is important to provide content in a culturally sensitive way to meet students where they are. Public-private partnerships can provide support, for example, to provide a financial structure that can incent talent to go into specific fields. The Federal Pell Grant Program could focus on science, technology, engineering, and mathematics (STEM) fields that the country needs by augmenting financial support to students who enroll in these fields, she suggested. She also stressed the importance of collaborations, noting groups with different areas of expertise can come together for better outcomes.

Ms. Ezediaro said the Bloomberg Foundation has a new portfolio focused on Black intergenerational wealth. "We are thinking about wealth building at the family, community, and institutional levels," she explained. "We want to interrupt systemic issues that cause students not to be prepared or have the resources they need at various points." While the specific intervention point has not been set, she said, the foundation is looking at how to fund community wealth models. The goal of the $100 million gift to the four medical schools, she added, is to give students more agency and choice in what they choose to specialize in. Students often make choices because they need to shorten their studies and earn an income sooner rather than later.

Dr. Iton identified critical junction points in the career trajectory of a "science-interested student," one of which is the period from the end of high school to the beginning of college. He suggested an expansion of resources during that time. He noted many bright students struggle and become intimidated by calculus or physical chemistry. They do not do well in those classes, then start to reconsider their choice. "There is such a squandering of talent when students run into the obstacles of calculus and chemistry," he said, "but there is an opportunity to support them and keep their appetite for science alive." Agreeing with Ms. Ezediaro's observation that many students of color need to start earning an income, he suggested one solution may be career "ladders" as pathways to health careers. "Let people get a foothold in the health-care field where they can get paid and acclimated to the environment, then continue as they become nurses, physician assistants, or physicians," he suggested. If they have "off ramps" to earn money, he added, they may hold on to science longer.

Dr. Hildreth noted that removing the intimidation factor requires students seeing role models, starting early in their schooling. As an example, he described a program at the University of California, Davis that teaches third graders to write computer code. He asked about other ideas for K–12 students. Dr. Iton replied that a point that emerged when looking at the K–12 STEM pipeline in California is that successful pathways programs have education, college, and employer components. He agreed that the educational component has to start young, and that expectations and a supporting infrastructure are required. Some programs struggle to keep African American men involved because of sports, he observed, and it is important to engage families to support their sons' participation in the programs.

Ms. Lezama called for a strategic focus and partnerships with experts in K–12 education. "We want to make sure every student has line of sight to a 4-year program," she said. NACME is in a collaboration called "Algebra by Seventh Grade."[1] Echoing Dr. Iton, she said calculus weeds out many students, and algebra leads up to calculus. One aspect of the partnership is to create information for parents to advocate for their children to get the math preparation they need.

Dr. Hildreth noted that HBCUs are producing fewer students who go on to medical school than in the past and said the infrastructure challenges in HBCUs must be addressed. When he asked how foundations, industry, and government could help, Dr. Iton replied, "This is about reparations. This is where the United States should invest its reparation dollars. Invest in opportunities for African Americans to repair the legacy of centuries of racism." He said without this investment, the same outcomes will persist. "We need the commitment to acknowledge, tell the truth, and heal," he stated. "HBCUs are a prime target for the investment necessary to bring about the repair."

Ms. Lezama called for a national strategy that allows the country to educate the excellence that exists in communities, including more support for HBCUs. Ms. Ezediaro added the focus should be on institutions that have had a history of systemic underinvestment. She noted that the four historically Black medical schools produce most of the nation's Black doctors yet are not key partners for many foundations.

Dr. Hildreth commented that the development of COVID-19 vaccines represents a "Sputnik moment" that shows what bold action can accomplish. "Something is calling out to us because of this moment, and we should not miss the opportunity," he urged. Drawing from history, Dr. Iton reminded the group that [in the early 1700s], Onesimus, an enslaved man in Massachusetts, explained the technology behind smallpox inoculations to Cotton Mather, a New England Puritan clergyman, yet the history of vaccination depicts the discovery as one of "white brilliance." He continued, "The narrative we have around African Americans in health in this country has been whitewashed. We need to change the narrative to change the policy. We have been at the leading edge of STEM, yet we hear that we are on the lagging edge. The narrative matters."

Ms. Lezama urged reshaping the cost of education. She noted that her daughter is a medical student at New York University, and the fact that she can graduate debt-free is huge.[2] Her daughter now has the expectation to work in an underrepresented area during her medical program, residency, and beyond. NACME is looking at how these models may apply in other fields so that financial barriers do not prevent entry. Ms. Ezediaro said many philanthropies have made commitments within the last year to think more deeply about equity. She acknowledged the work to be done in philanthropy to partner and learn what works, then to scale the programs that are working. She added that this includes how to get more people into the pipeline, as well as increase the representation in specific fields where more Black doctors are needed, such as cardiologists.

Dr. Hildreth asked the presenters about any changes in approaches they have seen in the context of greater realization about deep racial injustice. Ms. Lezama shared that the day after George Floyd's murder, she was contacted by allies who wanted to see what they could do. She noted that "structural racism did not change on that day, but what changed was the

---

[2] In 2018, the New York University School of Medicine announced free-tuition scholarships for medical students who maintain satisfactory academic progress. For more information, see https://med.nyu.edu/education/md-degree/md-affordability-financial-aid/cost-attendance.

realization of what African Americans experience on a regular basis." She urged the need "to be bold and leverage the opportunity. Use this moment in time to present the data and outcomes that if we invest, all will do better."

Dr. Iton added that most of his career has been in public health, where "the patient is the community." He commented that medical care only contributes about 15 percent to the health status of populations, with the rest occurring outside the doctor's office, shaped by structural racism. He noted that most Americans do not understand individual versus structural racism, while acknowledging the challenges in having these discussions. "I talk about racism a fair deal. We should name it and be straightforward. But we have to be cognizant that minds go to individual racism. Structural racism is racism without a clear racist," he said. Dr. Hildreth commented that part of his challenge at conferences where he is the only Black participant or when he was dean at the University of California, Davis has been to counter the belief that a diverse faculty could not be a quality faculty. Students cannot get excited about things they are not exposed to, and specialties with very low numbers of Black faculty perpetuate a situation of low numbers, Ms. Ezediaro said. She added that it is important not to hesitate to engage in controversial issues. Her portfolio focuses on intergenerational wealth for Black families, communities, and institutions, which means "the issues are not about today, they have been around for 400 plus years and at multiple levels." She agreed with Dr. Iton that "we do not have language to talk about race. There will be people who hear and turn way and minimize the opportunities of impact. This is the moment to step into the widest view and dedicate work for Black people," she stressed.

At the end of the session, the committee co-chairs summed up some of what was discussed during the workshop's first day. Dr. Theodore Corbin (Drexel University) underscored that "in this Sputnik moment, science is key to make a difference, and Black men and women are huge contributors." Dr. Barabino reflected that the conversations throughout the day built on the presentations by Dr. Raj Chetty (Harvard University) and Dr. Louis Sullivan (Sullivan Alliance). "This idea of what you start with and where you live—gaps between incomes, health, and wealth—is so stark," she commented. She agreed with Dr. Iton's point that African American stories need to "own the narrative." Dr. Sullivan commented there is more than one solution to address the problem of inadequate representation in STEM fields, but he returned to Dr. Chetty's research on the influence of location. He also said he found the engagement of the private sector encouraging. Dr. George Daley (Harvard Medical School) stressed the role of environment and importance of strong mentorship, including teaching mentorship skills. Dr. Corbin concluded with the need for radical solutions and bold ideas.

6

Beyond Finances: Living, Growing, and Thriving in Institutions of Higher Learning as a Standard

Highlights from the Presentations

- To counter students losing interest in or never becoming exposed to the potential of engineering, the Boston University (BU) Technology Innovation Scholars Program presents engineering careers as viable options for K–12 students and engages students in exciting engineering projects (Dr. Duncanson).
- It is important to create supportive spaces and a sense of community and not rely on only one or a very few Black faculty members in a department to support Black students (Dr. Duncanson).
- Creating a community of scholars at the undergraduate and graduate levels, through the Cardea Fellows Program and BioCoRE (Biosciences Collaborative for Research Engagement), have helped Black students persist in health and biomedical studies at Duke University (Ms. Cullins).
- Sustained support from high-level leadership is essential for programs to succeed (Ms. Cullins).
- Data, especially outcomes data, can be particularly useful to continue and maintain support for programs, but require financial and human resources to collect and analyze (Ms. Cullins, Dr. Ford).

- A holistic admissions process that looks at resilience, distance traveled, and mission fit, in addition to academics, has resulted in 34 percent of the University of California, Riverside (UCR) School of Medicine being composed of underrepresented minorities (Dr. Ford).
- Making the transition from a community college to the new environment of a 4-year institution can be challenging without support to bridge the gap (Dr. Ford).
- The E.E. Just Program at Dartmouth College embodies three principles: (1) mentorship and sponsorship, (2) inclusive community, and (3) intellectual engagement and professional development (Dr. Sutton).
- The concepts often front-loaded into introductory math courses merit examination, since these courses often serve as a gatekeeper to continuation in science, technology, engineering, and mathematics (STEM) fields (Dr. Sutton).

The second day of the workshop began with four presenters describing innovative programs to promote success for students at their institutions, moderated by Dr. Theodore Corbin (Drexel University). They were Wynter Duncanson, Ph.D. (Boston University), Maureen Cullins, A.M. (Duke University School of Medicine), Byron Ford, Ph.D. (University of California, Riverside School of Medicine), and Craig Sutton, Ph.D. (Dartmouth College).

BOSTON UNIVERSITY COLLEGE OF ENGINEERING

Dr. Duncanson discussed initiatives at BU's College of Engineering to reach students from underrepresented groups in Boston and worldwide, and she proposed structures and opportunities when considering pipelines.

She outlined the traditional pipeline from K–12 through a 4-year college degree, graduate school, postdoctoral training, and a faculty position. Looking at that pipeline, Black students are 3 percent of the nation's engineering faculty. Black students are awarded 1.5 percent of engineering doctoral degrees and 3.9 percent of engineering bachelor's degrees.

Dr. Duncanson suggested focusing on elementary, middle, and high school to answer the questions of why the number is so low and when students start to lose interest. She noted that the reasons underrepresented minorities often give relate to lack of role models, lack of awareness of what engineers do, beliefs that engineering is for white men, and an underlying fear of math and science.

Technology Innovation Scholars Program

The Technology Innovation Scholars Program (TISP) at BU is focused on K–12 outreach. She explained the goals of the program:

> We are striving to present engineering careers as viable options by promoting awareness of what engineers do, changing perceptions of who can do engineering, and providing relatable and engaging role models. Ultimately, we are aiming to increase interest in engineering by helping students do engineering, such as exciting engineering projects aligned to curriculum standards.

Current engineering majors are recruited to become "Inspiration Ambassadors" who go to middle and high schools in Boston and around the country to show how engineering can transform lives. She noted that studies have found that Black students are attracted to fields that have societal impacts, which dovetails with BU's priority to educate "societal engineers." The ambassadors are in their sophomore to senior years of college. They receive a small stipend ($1,200 annually) and culturally sensitive training. "They are committed to the goal of broadening representation in engineering," she explained. The 65 ambassadors are now 64 percent women and 36 percent men and represent different fields of engineering. Dr. Duncanson showed an excerpt of a video of a Black woman ambassador who explained her major, shared how she became interested in engineering, and described her pre-college classes and activities. Dr. Duncanson commented, "What I appreciate is that she is real and talks about when she became interested in STEM."

Innovations in a Box

To help K–12 students actually do engineering, BU students and faculty co-created "Innovations in a Box," which are interactive hands-on activities coupled with design challenges that span a class period of 45 or 90 minutes. They are based on faculty research. The innovations are used with groups and schools around Boston with high Black and Brown populations. Some students have gone on to take tours of BU laboratory facilities. During the pandemic, the program was conducted online and reached more students than previously. They have also expanded to grades 4 through 6 with a Lego Gadgets kit with which students build and code. Students are also exposed to the BU Robotics Laboratory.

To expand the impact, Dr. Duncanson said, the plan is to convert the "innovations" into kits to send into homes. She also urged deeper studies about loss of interest in engineering by Black students to learn what are the controllable factors, what existing policies limit access, and how outreach programs can close the gap.

DUKE UNIVERSITY SCHOOL OF MEDICINE

Ms. Cullins described two programs at Duke University School of Medicine, the Cardea Fellows Program on the undergraduate campus and Duke BioCoRE that works with Ph.D. and basic scientists. She began by noting,

> What we have all often heard when we talk about programs dealing with diversity, antiracism, and promoting the well-being of people of color is that the investment of leadership in these programs and the necessity of having good, strong leadership to promote the ethics and values need to be in place for these programs to thrive and continue.

She said the programs have been successful for the past 10 years because they had the investment of the dean, university president, and faculty when they began.

Cardea Fellows Program

The Cardea Fellows Program grew out of a summer program funded by the Robert Wood Johnson Foundation. Two participants of the program suggested that the program run a full year for students who are preparing or committed to a career in health care so that they can master core knowledge in math and science. The program encompasses specialized advising and support and also deals with curriculum and problems that cause students the most difficulty. For example, the math and chemistry departments decelerated some introductory courses to run over two semesters rather than one. "We are finding that once we have grounded students in the foundation, they are better able to master the upper-level sciences," she explained. "By decelerating calculus, they are ready for Physics 101 in a way they were not before."

When the Cardea Fellows Program started, she related, the campus newspaper labeled it a remedial program and wrote several articles criticizing it and the fellows. "We had to recast how the program was presented to the community and even to the students themselves," she recalled. To dispel these myths, students now apply to the program and the language about it explicitly says, "Every undergraduate admitted to Duke has demonstrated academic excellence." It took about 2 years to change the perception to show that the program is set up to prepare students' paths to achieve.

The program is structured so that students live together, participate in specialized advising and tutoring, meet weekly in a seminar to discuss issues they face, meet regularly with an academic advisor, and explore careers. More broadly, they are in a group of like-minded people with whom they can collaborate. They also have access to summer enrichment programs and receive free textbooks and supplementary resources for many pre-health courses.

In the tutoring program, which is called SAGE (STEM Advancement through Group Engagement), students meet weekly in small groups with trained peer facilitators. The facilitators are trained in academics as well as how to inoculate group members from diverging from their chosen paths. Duke deans and faculty recognize the Cardea Fellows as a premier program for highly motived students with strong interest in STEM learning and medicine. Faculty training of the peer facilitators is one reason for its success.

Duke BioCoRE

Duke BioCoRE began as a National Institutes of Health (NIH) initiative in which a supportive community of graduate students and faculty is built with opportunities for research, mentoring, and career development. Cardea Fellows and other undergraduates can also become part of BioCoRE and participate in longitudinal mentoring, research, and career development. The goal is to increase the diversity of scientists in biosciences. They gain a community across bioscience disciplines and departments, as their specialties can otherwise be lonely at the graduate level. "BioCoRE has impacted retention, happiness, and community engagement," she said.

She noted that the program covers diversity related to race, ethnicity, life experiences, religion, low wealth, and disabilities.

Another reason for success is creation of an office in the School of Medicine called IDEALS (Inclusion, Diversity, Equity, Advancement, and Leadership in the Sciences), led by Assistant Dean Johnna Frierson, Ph.D. IDEALS coordinates BioCoRE and also is engaged throughout the university. IDEALS takes on a large part of the antiracism work going on in the School of Medicine and is helping to apply a systems lens through which Duke creates programs, teaches the sciences, and engages students in their own learning and success.

Ms. Cullins concluded by noting that Duke has pathways programs for students beginning in the third grade on the undergraduate and graduate campuses.

UNIVERSITY OF CALIFORNIA, RIVERSIDE SCHOOL OF MEDICINE

Dr. Ford shared some programs at the University of California, Riverside School of Medicine (UCR SOM) to support the success of Black students. He reported that *U.S. News & World Report* ranked the school sixth in diversity; he added that this is the first year the magazine published a list of most diverse medical schools, which notes the importance that many institutions have placed on increasing minority access to medical education.

Intentional Diversity

The reason for the high ranking is intentional, he stated. Started in 2013 as a fully accredited medical school, the mission of UCR SOM is to improve the health of the people of California by training a diverse workforce of physicians and developing health-care delivery programs that will improve the health of the medically underserved in the region.

As discussed by Dr. Ford, the state as a whole is 59.5 percent white (36.6 percent non-Hispanic white), 14.7 percent Asian, 5.8 percent Black/African American. (Other races and Native Americans/Native Hawaiians/Pacific Islanders account for the rest of the population.) By ethnicity, 39.3 percent of California's total population is Hispanic-Latino. The medical school is 34 percent underrepresented minorities. A breakdown of UCR SOM's 299 students by race/ethnicity and gender (see Figure 6-1) shows that 7 percent of the students are Black/African American, which is consis-

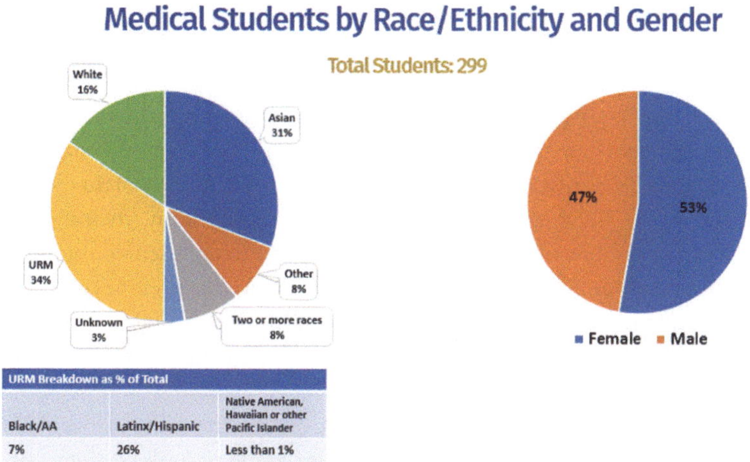

FIGURE 6-1 University of California, Riverside School of Medicine's composition by race and ethnic group.
SOURCE: Byron Ford, Workshop Presentation, April 20, 2021.

tent with the overall representation in the state's population. Dr. Ford noted that UCR SOM uses a holistic application review approach that, in addition to academic record, considers resilience, distance traveled, and mission fit. Of 198 medical students graduated so far, 156 have remained in California, including 59 who have remained in the state's Inland Empire region.

UCR's graduate programs also have greater diversity than the national average, Dr. Ford mentioned. Thirty-two percent of the current biomedical sciences graduate program are underrepresented minorities. Consistent with the medical school, about 7 percent are Black/African American and 23 percent are Latinx/Hispanic.

Riverside Bridges to the Baccalaureate Program and the UC-HBCU Initiative Program

Dr. Ford serves as co-principal investigator for the NIH-funded Riverside Bridges to the Baccalaureate (Riverside B2B) Program along with Wolde-Ab Isaac, the chancellor of Riverside City College (RCC). With buy-in from Dr. Isaac and others in RCC's top leadership, the partnership provides underrepresented students with resources to transition from RCC to research-oriented STEM programs at UCR. "In many cases, students graduate with their associate degrees and then join an entirely new environment as juniors and have to connect with a new environment," he pointed out. UCR leaders and representatives of different pipeline programs visit RCC to make students aware of the resources to which they have access when they transfer. For example, a summer research program brings RCC students to UCR research laboratories. Eleven RCC B2B students recently transferred to UCR through the program, nine of whom (including two Black students now working in SOM labs) are underrepresented minorities. He noted that an informal poll showed that despite the proximity to UCR, RCC students did not necessarily plan to transfer there because they did not feel welcome. All the students in the program have chosen UCR as their top choice.

The UC-HBCU (Historically Black Colleges and Universities) initiative is based on data that African Americans made up only 2.8 percent of the students enrolled across all University of California academic doctoral programs between 2010 and 2015. Dr. Ford describe how the UC Office of the President launched the program to improve diversity and strengthen UC graduate programs by investing in strong collaborations between UC faculty and HBCUs. These are active collaborations, not just "coming to an HBCU to harvest students," Dr. Ford stressed. As part of the initiative, Dr. Ford received a grant entitled Pathways to Biomedical Science and Neuroscience to establish a partnership with Morehouse College, Fort Valley State University, Spelman College, and Morehouse School of Medicine. UC-HBCU students accepted in the UC system receive a fully funded fellowship for 5 years.

Challenges, Barriers, and Solutions

Dr. Ford identified the need for increased local, regional, and national support for diversity programs, especially for universities to create an infrastructure so that faculty can apply for these programs. At the forefront of discussions at UCR is the need to improve recruitment and especially retention of Black faculty. A prioritization of research in health equity and social justice is needed, as is addressing systemic bias and racism in academic institutions. "We've started to have those courageous conversations at UCR about how we address this," he said. Reflecting the suggestion of other presenters, he concluded, "This is the time we should strike while the iron is hot. We should be bold in our asks."

DARTMOUTH COLLEGE

Dr. Sutton described the E.E. Just Program at Dartmouth College. Ernest Everett Just was a Phi Beta Kappa graduate of Dartmouth in 1907 and a pioneering African American cell biologist. Dr. Sutton also considered some broader questions that the program helps raise.

E.E. Just Program

Although the program has existed for several decades, it underwent a new iteration in 2012 to increase the number of underrepresented minorities at Dartmouth who pursue degrees and careers in STEM. The program is built on three core values: (1) mentorship and sponsorship, (2) inclusive community, and (3) intellectual engagement and professional development. "When these values are put into motion, they take the shape of community building through intellectual cross-pollination, and mentorship and opportunity at critical transition points," Dr. Sutton said.

Community building occurs through three programs open to everyone on campus. E.E. Just Jam Sessions meet weekly for STEM undergraduates and graduates to engage in intellectual improvisations and discover unexpected connections; for example, a short presentation might take place followed by breakout sessions facilitated by E.E. Just Graduate Mentors. The E.E. Just Science Forum brings undergraduate and graduate students together for a short dinner presentation by faculty members, visiting scientists, and E.E. Just Interns and Fellows. They are intended to introduce the community to a variety of ideas at the frontiers of science. The E.E. Just Science Symposium is a weekend-long conference with talks from experts in a myriad of STEM disciplines.

With these programs creating the general atmosphere, the program also has mentorship and opportunities at critical transition points, Dr. Sutton continued. In a previous iteration, students applied for and were selected for a 4-year program, but this model was not the best fit for a liberal arts environment. Instead, the current program with on and off ramps was developed, beginning with Dartmouth Adventures in STEM (DAS). Dr. Sutton described DAS as a weeklong pre-orientation program that introduces students to the frontiers of science through minicourses taught by Dartmouth professors about their research and community-building activities. DAS is designed to foster an intellectually and socially cohesive incoming cohort, not so much skills acquisition as getting students excited about STEM. "We found this has had several effects. When students are entering college, there is usually some hesitation about being intellectually vulnerable with one another," he said. Rather than offering a class in a subject that some students will already have taken, research scientists come in and talk about what they do and, as Dr. Sutton characterized it, "create a state of confusion for everyone." In this state of confusion, students band together and see each other as collaborators. "It helps lower inhibitions about being intellectually vulnerable and creates a strong cohort of entering students," Dr. Sutton said.

Another touchpoint in the E.E. Just Program are two internships with faculty, one after students' first year on campus and the other at the Marine Biological Laboratory at the Woods Hole Oceanographic Institute, where Dr. Just spent part of his career.

The E.E. Just Undergraduate Fellowship Program is modeled after the Mellon Mays Undergraduate Fellowship Program in the humanities.[1] Sophomores can receive 2 years of funding to conduct research year-round under the supervision of a faculty member, which is designed to culminate in a senior thesis and prepare them for graduate school. They also participate in professional development.

The final stage is programs for graduate students, Dr. Sutton described. The E.E. Just Liftoff Fellowship is designed for first-year graduate students to receive professional development and form an inclusive community of budding scholars. E.E. Just Graduate Fellows are senior graduate students who mentor undergraduate and first-year graduate members of the community and help facilitate programmatic activities, such as the Jams mentioned above.

Wider Implications

The implications for Dartmouth and other institutions relate to community, mentorship, and curriculum, Dr. Sutton said. Community is very important and has increased the retention rate of STEM students. However, it also raises the question for the academy about what community means and how to cultivate it. "It's one thing to have a place where underrepresented minorities can go to feel included, but how do we make that the default experience on campus?" he queried.

---

[1] For information on the Mellon Mays Undergraduate Fellowship Program, see https://www.mmuf.org/.

Dr. Sutton stressed that a cadre of mentors is needed, but effective mentorship is a skill that must be cultivated by universities, not left to chance. He suggested universities think how they can be more intentional in supporting mentoring and creating a professoriate for the 21st century that adds value to the community and to the traditional research and teaching portfolio, and that should include mentorship.

Related to curriculum, as a mathematician he has observed that math courses often serve as the gatekeeper for students interested in STEM. "Are our introductory sequences disrupting inequities that we already know exist in K–12, or are they reinforcing and perpetuating them?" he asked. He urged the attendees and participants to rethink how to introduce math to students and asked a series of questions: Is calculus the right first course? If so, should it be taught in a different way? Can introductory sequences capture the imagination of students by highlighting current problems while laying out a foundation for future work? He noted when he chaired a committee to look at the math curriculum, he went to different departments to ask how students use math in their disciplines. Many things expressed as a need are not used. He suggested that every concept does not have to be front-loaded in an introductory calculus class, but instead taught when students really need to use it.

DISCUSSION

The programs are remarkable and important, Dr. Corbin reflected. He asked how behavioral and mental health are addressed in them. Dr. Ford replied that UCS SOM realized these aspects of health have to be embedded in all that is done. Figuring out how to operate during COVID-19 and holding town halls during the Black Lives Matter protests showed the importance of health and wellness. Black students felt extremely stressed. It was critical to figure out how to reach out to faculty and students and create community. Ms. Cullins said conversations on these issues are ongoing. Her office found that students need reassurance when the environment is in upheaval, she said. "What helped us was finally getting the chancellor, the president, and the dean together to communicate with the students and make sure resources were available," she said.

Dr. George Daley (Harvard Medical School) commented about the many references to the importance of community, which goes to the issue of a community's critical mass to contribute to a sense of belonging. An issue in Boston is that it is not considered a welcoming community, he observed.

He said Harvard Medical School has tried to "create a community within a community that can create a sense of belonging, but we are challenged." Dr. Duncanson said that "being the only one" is a problem. They will be the person that all of the Black students go to. One or two Black faculty members are not enough, she stressed, and spaces where people can be together is also important. Dr. Sutton said at the student level, Dartmouth is creating a space on campus to build community across disciplines, which also potentially produces scientists with a more interdisciplinary outlook. At the faculty and staff level, it is difficult for institutions in rural areas like northern New England, he acknowledged. However, he suggested that something that could stem the flow from such locations is when institutions come out unabashedly in favor of "effecting the type of change we are talking about." Underrepresented minority students typically want to have social impact, as do faculty and staff, Dr. Sutton noted. In his view, influential institutions can have a huge impact if they are fully committed to change. Dr. Daley suggested that cluster hires, now being undertaken at Harvard Medical School and which NIH recently supported in its For Inspiration and Recognition of Science and Technology, or FIRST, program, may be an effective way to ensure more faculty of color at an institution. Dr. Ford said a roadblock to community building is an institution's perception of itself versus what students and others think of it. UCR, he said, considers itself "the diversity school of the UC system," but students do not always see it as inviting as it sees itself. Important conversations must take place internally, he urged, so perception is consistent with what others see.

A participant asked how the programs prepare students to respond to microaggressions and macroaggressions. Dr. Ford said the first thing is to educate the entire campus, including training the trainers. They may attempt to improve the environment for students of color, but have not themselves necessarily been appropriately trained. UCR SOM has a new thread called the "health, equity, social justice, and anti-racism thread" throughout its 4-year curriculum. The intent is to reinforce that these concepts should be part of medical care, mentoring students, and incorporated in all that physicians do, and not just be "set up as a web-based training course."

Dr. Duncanson said at the undergraduate level, BU is infusing aspects of diversity and inclusion in all engineering courses to see the consequences of not including all voices and to consider "How can we be more inclusive in the way we engineer?" Ms. Cullins described a longitudinal course at Duke's School of Medicine that deals with health disparities and aggressions. Faculty are rotating through an 8-week course entitled "Teach Equity Now" that deals with the history of racism and white supremacy, then discusses how to incorporate the concepts in whatever course they teach or job they perform. She noted that the school's pipeline programs for younger students now admit cohorts so that they do not go back home as "the only."

Dr. Daley said the Learning Environment Committee at Harvard Medical School was initially formed to address responses on the school's graduate questionnaire about mistreatment. They have found that an approach to antiracism training that draws from patient safety training is helpful. Dr. Sutton expressed hope that such training becomes the default way to onboard all faculty and staff and that a citizenship portfolio, in addition to teaching and research portfolios, become a standard consideration in tenure and promotion. He urged being intentional about people needing to recognize implicit bias and have related skills as they progress through the ranks. "How can we move from 'it would be nice if you did these workshops' to 'this is that you need to know in a 21st century university'?" he asked. Dr. Daley noted that the medical community requires continuing medical education, so there could be piggybacking on this system of training and validation by instituting implicit bias and other training.

Dr. Ford said UCR SOM students do not report experiencing aggressions at the school, but there have been some issues at hospitals where they train. They are establishing efforts to strengthen site comparability through faculty development and onboarding. Mentors, both new and veteran, will need to go through training to understand the needs of current students.

As the formal discussion closed, several panelists highlighted their institutions' work with K–12 schools and the importance of data. Ms. Cullins described a program at Duke called BOOST (Building Opportunities and Overtures in Science and Technology) that starts with students in the fourth grade. They are nominated by their teachers and are on free and reduced lunch. All of the students in BOOST have graduated high school, and 30 to 40 percent have gone on to college. Dr. Duncanson said BU will analyze the impact of outreach on students through the school's new Racial Data Lab. Dr. Ford underscored the need for data on outcomes. UCR has many pipeline programs, but it is difficult to continue and maintain support for them, especially for the federal government, without outcome data. An infrastructure is needed so that faculty, particularly faculty of color, can do this work but also attend to their own research and careers. Ms. Cullins commented that Duke recently pulled together its pathway programs across the Schools of Medicine and Nursing into one office. A director and assistant director were hired, with money to support data collection and analysis. She noted that foundations also want to see data. Grants often do not provide enough funds for evaluation and tracking, she added, and the institution needs to use its own resources to accomplish this.

7

Policies, Programs, and Resources

Highlights from the Presentations

- Legislation to promote the progress of women and minorities in science, technology, engineering, and mathematics (STEM) is needed to take advantage of the creativity and imagination that exist in those communities (Rep. Johnson).
- Independent funding for students provides them with the freedom to chart their own course, rather than be constrained by the principal investigator in their laboratories (Dr. McMurry-Heath).
- A key to connecting policies, programs, and resources is to make visible what is invisible related to bias and inequity (Dr. McMurry-Heath).
- It is important not just to arm students to be resilient but also disarm opposition (Dr. McMurry-Heath).
- The collaboration between the Roundtable on Black Men and Black Women in Science, Engineering, and Medicine's Finance and Public Engagement action groups underscores how these two themes are interrelated (Dr. Daley).
- A systems change, not a one-off solution, is required for lasting impact (Dr. Sullivan).
- Now is the time to think big and seize the momentum (Dr. Barabino).

- To impact lives earlier, a mentorship curriculum should be a standard throughout every facet of education and the Departments of Education and Health and Human Services should work together to develop solutions around public education (Dr. Corbin).

The final session of the workshop featured brief remarks from Rep. Eddie Bernice Johnson (TX-30) about the importance of Black participation in STEM careers and legislative action to help promote it. Planning co-chair Gilda Barabino, Ph.D. (Olin College of Engineering), and Michelle McMurry-Heath, M.D., Ph.D. (Biotechnology Innovation Organization), then conversed about how policies, programs, and resources intersect in increasing Black participation in science, engineering, and medicine. The session closed with final reflections from the planning committee and Roundtable chairs.

CONGRESSIONAL PERSPECTIVE: REP. EDDIE BERNICE JOHNSON

Congresswoman Johnson reaffirmed her commitment to increasing the participation of Black students in STEM education and expressed her belief that the well-being and success of future generations depend on it. She noted that she has introduced legislation to promote the progress of women and minorities in STEM careers. "It is often at the heart of these communities that creativity and imagination lie, and we must ensure those students have an outlet to express their talents," she stated. "As the first woman and first African American chair of the Science, Space, and Technology Committee in the U.S. House of Representatives, I will continue to advocate for a strong diverse STEM workforce."

"FIRESIDE CHAT": DR. GILDA BARABINO AND DR. MICHELLE MCMURRY-HEATH

Dr. Barabino explained her conversation with Dr. McMurry-Heath was designed to better understand the interrelatedness of policies, programs, and resources in supporting Black scientists, engineers, and medical professionals. She noted that sessions throughout the workshop recognized that disparities and opportunity gaps exist and that policies are needed to create the conditions to address these disparities and close gaps. The issues are not new, she acknowledged, referring to an article that Roundtable member Shirley Malcom, Ph.D., wrote 25 years ago entitled "Science and Diversity: A Compelling National Interest" (Malcom, 1996). In that article, which appeared in *Science*, Dr. Malcom wrote of the continued threat to the progress of Blacks in science absent strategic use of policies, programs, and resources, and the need for structural changes backed by policies. "A quarter-century later, those sentiments ring true," Dr. Barabino said. "We need to seize the moment for an investment in Black talent as a compelling national interest."

Dr. Barabino introduced Dr. McMurry-Heath as a champion for access to scientific progress as a social justice issue throughout her career spanning academia, government, and industry. Asked what drew her to policy, Dr. McMurry-Health said her parents were public health leaders in Oakland, California, and she grew up seeing the intersection of policy and medicine. In finding her own way to contribute, she saw laboratory-based science as key. At Harvard University as an undergraduate, 3 years working at the bench in addition to classes showed her a "whole privileged world that provided the opportunity to ask scientific questions in a way that could improve health that was hidden from the communities where I had grown up." She said she made it her mission to inform both sides of the equation: scientists and communities. At Duke University, she enrolled in policy courses that made her consider such questions as who determines which projects are funded, what scientists owe taxpayers for providing public support, and how social factors influence patient care. "I've been asking these questions for 20 years," she continued. "It's been about trying to make sure the science gets done, but it is also key that communities see the power that science can offer them."

Dr. Barabino observed that many students of color want to give back to the community and solve problems, but some are discouraged from taking time from their research. Dr. McMurry-Health said a UNCF (United Negro College Fund) fellowship, in addition to a National Institutes of Health (NIH) fellowship, provided her with independence. "That kind of academic freedom allowed me to ask the questions that were most important to me in addition to the questions that were most important to my PI [principal investigator]," she said. "I hope we find a way to give that kind of independence to more students." She acknowledged the pressures on students and noted students may question if they are making a difference or ever will while they are in the process of laboratory-based science training. "If we don't help those students stay connected to that mission and purpose, we will lose them," she said.

Dr. Barabino asked Dr. McMurry-Heath to elaborate on the connection between policies, programs, and the resources to support them. "It starts with leadership's intention to have an impact and make change," Dr. McMurry-Heath replied. "We have to realize that students are under a lot of social pressure. Anything we can do to help liberate them from these forces and connect with each other will go a long way toward their eventual success." Independent funding to students provides them flexibility and independence if they do not connect with their principal investigator, if their family circumstances change, or if they want to change course for another reason. More could be done with NIH to demonstrate the value of finding diverse solutions to critical problems and being inclusive in research, she suggested. She applauded NIH's recent proposal to rate diversity in some grant proposals.[1]

"We need to make visible what is not being seen," Dr. Barabino said. "We need to use our voices." In this regard, she asked Dr. McMurry-Health about a study she undertook of National Science Foundation policies, programs, and personnel applicable to the workshop themes. Dr. McMurry-Heath said what was clear in this "deep dive" was the importance of providing graduate students a living wage. Studies show poor and minority students are more likely to also be first-generation scientists and have a lack of clarity about what science offers for their future. Giving students the tools to live and progress is important, she stressed. She added that what sometimes gets neglected are the increasing rates of infertility and maternal mortality among Black women, many of whom are delaying childbearing to remain in training programs, another example of making the invisible visible.

Dr. Barabino commented on the need for greater access to opportunities. Dr. McMurry-Heath said her views have shifted—before 2020, she said she would have stressed the need to build more resilient students interested in STEM, reflecting on the successful work of Freeman Hrabowski III, Ph.D., at the University of Maryland, Baltimore County. However, she asserted, "another side that the events of 2020 opened our eyes to and made the invisible visible is *why* are we depending on young souls to be so resilient?" She noted the pressure she felt at Duke to succeed as a Black scientist and stressed:

[1] See, for example, NIH Notice Number NOT-OD-22-019: Reminder: Notice of NIH's Encouragement of Applications Supporting Individuals from Underrepresented Ethnic and Racial Groups as well as Individuals with Disabilities.

> What we need to focus on is not just arming youth, but disarming opposition. We need to find ways that medical training and scientific training are less of an affront to the sensibilities, the values, and the experiences of so many of the young people in our community. That will aid in access because the admissions rate, the criteria selection, the welcome mat are all dialed down by some of those headwinds. We need to ask ourselves, What's driving that and how can we dismantle it?

Dr. Barabino noted that the workshop discussions centered on the need not only to strengthen individuals but also to work on institutional transformation, systems, and structures to make a difference. Another area shown to make a difference is mentorship, but it is contextual, she added. Dr. McMurry-Heath concurred that mentorship is key, but she also called attention to a concept she did not learn until the middle of her career at Johnson & Johnson: sponsorship. "In the private sector, it is common to talk not just about mentorship to impart skills and information but also about sponsorship in which someone is advocating for you behind closed doors," she explained. She stressed the need for mentors and sponsors to break open paths. In addition, a kind word at the right time makes a difference. She recalled looking for a job in Washington, D.C., with little success, when Dr. Vivian Pinn (first full-time director of the NIH Office of Research on Women's Health) responded with a handwritten letter. She did not have a role for Dr. McMurry-Heath, but encouraged her to keep trying. "That was what I needed to keep pursuing my goal," Dr. McMurry-Heath recalled. "As we progress in our careers, we have to keep an eye out for burgeoning talent who are often struggling with decision points. They are pulled in different directions. Giving them support to help them make decisions that are their True North is very important."

Dr. McMurry-Health returned to the theme of making the invisible visible. "The more we can make up-and-coming minority clinicians and scientists and engineers visible to youth behind them, the more success they will have," she commented. She recognized the need to avoid pulling Black professionals in many different directions—doing double or triple duty when they are expected to represent every minority cause while also doing their bench work—but making their accomplishments visible.

Referring to the "dueling pandemics" of COVID-19 and systemic racism, Dr. Barabino asked how to seize momentum to make a difference. As an example, Dr. McMurry-Heath noted that her first full week as CEO of BIO (Biotechnology Innovation Organization) coincided with the organization's annual conference and the funeral of George Floyd. Public dialogue within the organization led to development of the BIO Equality Agenda. She described its three tenets. The first is to fight for inclusive clinical trials and diverse access to therapies, using COVID-19 as a test case. The second is making talent visible, including making sure investments by large companies are seen across the board. As an example, BIO is building a LinkedIn network of alumni of training programs across companies so that their skills and experience are visible throughout the ecosystem. She noted this is important not just for individuals but also for small biotech companies. The third is using the "power of the purse." BIO members are huge purchasers of equipment, goods, and services, and these represent opportunities to "purchase with a conscience," Dr. McMurry-Heath noted. A BIO program allows small companies to purchase at group rates, and the program is starting to show which suppliers have prioritized diversity and/or are minority led. She noted that the program has been very positively received throughout the organization.

Dr. Barabino asked Dr. McMurry-Heath to expand on her belief that "science is the social justice issue of our age." Dr. McMurry-Heath replied, "If we look at key levers for poverty reduction and opportunity expansion, it is things like clean air and water, access to nutritious food for children, and freedom from illness. All can be resolved or mitigated by science." She noted some examples of companies that are developing technologies that can make a difference in communities and in health-care delivery.

Dr. McMurry-Heath lauded the Roundtable for putting a spotlight on the issues discussed. She cautioned, however, that "what keeps me up at night—and what I hope folks will focus on—is backsliding. As we go forward, we have to be vigilant and prevent backlash."

CLOSING REMARKS

The planning committee co-chairs shared some takeaways they learned from the workshop. Dr. George Daley (Harvard Medical School) noted the workshop was co-organized by the Roundtable's Public Engagement and Finance action groups, and those two themes were interwoven throughout the sessions. From a financial perspective, he pointed out, debt is a major barrier to higher education for Black scientists and physicians (see Chapter 4). He said he was encouraged by major gifts like that of the Bloomberg Foundation (see Chapter 5), but more needs to be done in both medicine and other science and engineering fields to augment graduate stipends. Related to public education, many speakers stressed the importance of engagement of Black clinicians and scientists as role models, mentors, and persons; of diversifying faculties to have more role models; and of providing enrichment at all levels. Drawing on the importance of early interventions discussed by Dr. Raj Chetty (Harvard University) (see Chapter 2), Dr. Daley said he is compelled to think about how to engage and inspire students starting at the youngest ages. Having a bigger impact on policy is needed, and he urged finding a way to use the Roundtable to influence government policy.

Dr. Sullivan commented that philanthropic contributions to Historically Black Colleges and Universities (HBCUs) and medical schools occurred because of donor interest. "What I come away with is that there is a level of interest among those who have resources to see where they can fit in," he commented. "For the Roundtable, what I would like to see is not a one-off response, but a systems change." He suggested that Roundtable members engage with leaders through the Business Roundtable, Council on Foundations, U.S. Congress, and the President's Cabinet to work together as active problem solvers. "We should be able to find solutions and find ways to communicate with each other," he said. "This is the time for us to have big actions and major responses."

Dr. Barabino also noted the increase in philanthropic support and urged the Roundtable to take a leadership role in advising how to invest the resources. She reminded the group of Dr. Chetty's findings that interventions will not have lasting impacts unless external forces that serve as barriers are removed. Referring to his comments about segregation, she noted that some people generationally talk about what was lost with integration, such as Black businesses and doctors. She asked how to avoid the harm of segregation while maintaining the resources that can keep a community together.

Dr. Theodore Corbin (Drexel University) referred to Dr. Chetty's call for investments in housing, education, and other services. He pointed out the opportunity of the Roundtable to act as a convener and referred to the need, as discussed by Dr. Barabino and Dr. McMurry-Heath, to make visible what is invisible. Dr. Corbin also noted the need for a mentorship curriculum as a standard throughout every facet of education and the potential impact to work with the Departments of Education and Health and Human Services to develop solutions for public education. Roundtable member Dr. Shirley Malcom stressed the need for a place-based strategy to support housing, arts, economic development, health, food, and other areas. This strategy could be taken to community-based foundations that invest locally, she suggested.

Dr. Daley commented that the chat with Dr. McMurry-Heath brought out many issues. "Now we have to go out there and get things done," he said. Dr. Louis Sullivan (Sullivan Alliance) concluded that the big problems in society are solvable, and "we are the people who should be taking the lead in solving them. Everyone has a role to play, and we can serve to facilitate the connections." Dr. Cato Laurencin (Roundtable chair) thanked the participants and closed out the workshop by commenting on the great ideas that came out of it, including the need to create lasting solutions.

REFERENCE

Malcom, S. 1996. Science and diversity: A compelling national interest. *Science* 271(5257): 1817–1819.

Appendix A

Workshop Agenda

REDUCING FINANCIAL BARRIERS FOR BLACK STUDENTS IN SCIENCE, ENGINEERING, AND MEDICINE: A WORKSHOP

April 19–20, 2021
9:30 AM–5:00 PM EST

9:30 AM EST Opening Remarks and Introductions

Victor Dzau, M.D., President, National Academy of Medicine
Cato T. Laurencin, M.D., Ph.D., Chair of the Roundtable
Co-chairs of the Finance and Public Engagement Action Groups
Gilda Barabino, Ph.D.
George Q. Daley, M.D., Ph.D.
Theodore Corbin, M.D., M.P.P.
Louis Sullivan, M.D.
Marc Nivet, Ed.D.

SESSION I: TALENT ACQUISITION/ BEING A PROBLEM-SOLVING SOCIETY

Moderator: **George Q. Daley, M.D., Ph.D.**

10:00 AM Presentations

Session Objectives:

Update on the current state of affairs for Blacks/African Americans in the health professions and science and engineering fields. Understand the Black-white wealth gap and how this impedes progress of African Americans in science-related careers. Describe the historical context of the impact on federal funding in support of African Americans pursuing a career in medicine, science, and engineering fields. Highlight best practices of financial support of college students interested in careers in medicine and engineering.

Louis Sullivan, M.D.
Raj Chetty, Ph.D.

11:00 AM Q&A

SESSION II: ENGAGING PUBLIC TO IMPART CHANGE

Moderator: **Theodore Corbin, M.D., M.P.P.**

11:30 AM Presentations

Session Objectives:

Explore solutions that worked in the past to build and invest in Black students pursuing careers in science, engineering, and medicine. Promotion of policies to ensure the support of programs for science, engineering, and medicine. Identify the power/authoritative entities to make change.

David Satcher, M.D., Ph.D.
Sonsiere Cobb-Souza

12:30 PM Q&A

1:00 PM–1:30 PM Break for Lunch

SESSION III: CREATING OPPORTUNITIES FOR THE FUTURE

Moderator: **Theodore Corbin, M.D., M.P.P.**

1:30 PM Presentations

Session Objectives:

Examine the opportunities to eliminate debt burden while exploring the opportunities and contingencies in science engineering and medicine for Black men and Black women. The panelists will discuss the efforts taking place at their respective institutions/organizations and across the country.

Geoffery Young, Ph.D.
Sylvester James Gates Jr., Ph.D.
Garth Graham, M.D., Ph.D.

2:30 PM Q&A

SESSION IV: FELLOWSHIPS, PHILANTHROPY, AND INDUSTRY

Moderator: **James Hildreth, M.D., Ph.D.**

3:00 PM Presentations

Session Objectives:

Explore the role of industry, foundation, and philanthropic financing to advance the goal of greater diversity and inclusion in science, engineering, and medicine fields. The speakers will review the progress to date and how their specific interventions endeavor to change the landscape for the future, with highlights on measurable outcomes and objectives.

Garnesha Ezediaro (Bloomberg Foundation)
Michele Lezama, M.S., M.B.A. (NACME)
Anthony B. Iton, M.D., J.D., M.P.H. (California Endowment)

4:00 PM Discussion with Roundtable Members

4:30 PM Final Thoughts of the Day (Co-chair Remarks)

5:00 PM Day One Adjourned

DAY TWO

SESSION V: LIVE, GROW, AND THRIVE IN INSTITUTIONS OF HIGHER LEARNING AS A STANDARD

Moderator: **Theodore Corbin, M.D., M.P.P.**

1:15 PM Presentations

Session Objectives:

Speak to the innovative programs and processes in institutions to promote success in Black students interested in science, engineering, and medicine. The panelists will describe the unique programs that support such success in Black students.

Maureen Cullins, A.M.
Wynter Duncanson, Ph.D.
Craig Sutton, Ph.D.
Byron Ford, Ph.D.

QUESTIONS:

What are your best practices and outcomes? What lessons can be learned for scaling?

2:15 PM Discussion

2:45 PM Break

SESSION VI: THE POLICIES, PROGRAMS, AND RESOURCES

Moderator: **Gilda Barabino, Ph.D.**

3:00 PM "Fireside Chat" with Michelle McMurry-Heath, M.D., Ph.D.

3:45 PM Remarks from Rep. Eddie Bernice Johnson

4:00 PM Closing Discussion and Remarks

4:30 PM Day Two Adjourn

Appendix B

Biographical Sketches of Roundtable Members and Speakers

(In order of workshop appearance)

Victor J. Dzau, M.D., is the president of the National Academy of Medicine (NAM), formerly the Institute of Medicine (IOM). In addition, he serves as vice chair of the National Research Council. Dr. Dzau is chancellor emeritus and James B. Duke Professor of Medicine at Duke University and the past president and CEO of the Duke University Health System. Previously, Dr. Dzau was the Hershey Professor of Theory and Practice of Medicine and chairman of medicine at Harvard Medical School's Brigham and Women's Hospital, as well as chairman of the Department of Medicine at Stanford University.

He is an internationally acclaimed leader and scientist whose work has improved health care in the United States and globally. His seminal work in cardiovascular medicine and genetics laid the foundation for the development of the class of lifesaving drugs known as ACE inhibitors, used globally to treat hypertension and heart failure. Dr. Dzau pioneered gene therapy for vascular disease and was the first to introduce DNA decoy molecules to block transcriptions in humans in vivo. His pioneering research in cardiac regeneration led to the Paracrine Hypothesis of stem cell action and his recent strategy of direct cardiac reprogramming using microRNA. He maintains an active National Institutes of Health (NIH)–funded research laboratory.

In his role as a leader in health care, Dr. Dzau has led efforts in innovation to improve health, including the development of the Duke Translational Medicine Institute, the Duke Global Health Institute, the Duke–National University of Singapore Graduate Medical School, and the Duke Institute for Health Innovation. He has served as a member of the Advisory Committee to the Director at NIH, chaired the NIH Cardiovascular Disease Advisory Committee, and currently chairs the NIH Cardiovascular Stem Cell Biology and Translational Consortia. Currently, he is a member of the Board of the Singapore Health System, member of the Health Biomedical Sciences International Advisory Council of Singapore and Advisory Council of the Imperial College Health Partners, UK. He chairs the International Scientific Advisory Committee of the Qatar Genome Project, chairs the Scientific Boards of the Peter Munk Cardiac Center, University of Toronto, and Institute of Cardiovascular and Medical Sciences, University of Glasgow. He was on the Canada Gairdner Award Medical Advisory Board and is now on the Board of Directors of the Gairdner Foundation. He served on the Board of Health Governors of the World Economic Forum and chaired its Global Agenda Council on Precision Medicine.

Since arriving at the National Academies of Sciences, Engineering, and Medicine, Dr. Dzau has designed and led important initiatives such as the Commission on a Global Health Risk Framework for the Future; the Human Genome Editing Initiative; and Vital Directions for Health and Health Care. The launch of the NAM Grand Challenge for Healthy Longevity represents his vision to inspire across disciplines and sectors to coalesce around a shared priority and audacious goal to advance health.

Among his many honors and recognitions are the Max Delbrück Medal from Charite, Humboldt and Max Planck, Germany, the Distinguished Scientist Award from the American Heart Association, Ellis Island Medal of Honor, and the Henry Freisen International Prize. In 2014, he received the Public Service Medal from the president of Singapore. He has been elected to the National Academy of Medicine, the American Academy of Arts and Sciences, the European Academy of Sciences and Arts, and Academia Sinica. He has received 16 honorary doctorates.

Cato T. Laurencin, M.D., Ph.D., *(Chair)* **(NAM, NAE)** is the University Professor and Albert and Wilda Van Dusen Distinguished Endowed Professor of Orthopaedic Surgery at the University of Connecticut (UConn). He is professor of chemical engineering, professor of materials science and engineering, and professor of biomedical engineering at the school. He serves as the CEO of the Connecticut Convergence Institute for Translation in Regenerative Engineering and the director of the Raymond and

Beverly Sackler Center for Biomedical, Biological, Physical and Engineering Sciences at UConn.

Dr. Laurencin earned a B.S.E. in chemical engineering from Princeton University, and his M.D., magna cum laude, from the Harvard Medical School, and received the Robinson Award for Surgery. He earned his Ph.D. in biochemical engineering/biotechnology from the Massachusetts Institute of Technology, where he was named a Hugh Hampton Young Fellow. A practicing sports medicine and shoulder surgeon, Dr. Laurencin has been named to America's Top Doctors for more than 15 years. He is a Fellow of the American Academy of Orthopaedic Surgeons, a Fellow of the American Orthopaedic Association, a Fellow of the American College of Surgeons, and a member of the American Surgical Association. He received the Nicolas Andry Award, the highest honor of the Association of Bone and Joint Surgeons. Dr. Laurencin served as dean of the Medical School and vice president for health affairs at the University of Connecticut.

Dr. Laurencin is a pioneer of the new field regenerative engineering. He is an expert in biomaterials science, stem cell technology, and nanotechnology and was named one of the 100 Engineers of the Modern Era by the American Institute of Chemical Engineers. He received the Founder's Award (highest award) from the Society for Biomaterials, the Von Hipple Award (highest award) from the Materials Research Society, and the James Bailey Award (highest award) from the Society for Biological Engineering. He received the National Institutes of Health Director's Pioneer Award, NIH's highest and most prestigious research award, for his new field of regenerative engineering and the National Science Foundation's Emerging Frontiers in Research and Innovation Grant Award. Dr. Laurencin is the editor-in-chief of *Regenerative Engineering and Translational Medicine*, published by Springer Nature, and is the founder of the Regenerative Engineering Society. He is a Fellow of the American Chemical Society, a Fellow of the American Institute of Chemical Engineers, a Fellow of the Biomedical Engineering Society, a Fellow of the Materials Research Society, and an American Association for the Advancement of Science (AAAS) Fellow. The AAAS awarded Dr. Laurencin the Philip Hauge Abelson Prize given "for signal contributions to the advancement of science in the United States."

Dr. Laurencin is active in mentoring, especially underrepresented minority students. He received the AAAS Mentor Award, the Beckman Award for Mentoring, and the Presidential Award for Excellence in Science, Mathematics, and Engineering Mentoring in ceremonies at the White House. The Society for Biomaterials established the Cato T. Laurencin,

MD, PhD Travel Fellowship in his honor, awarded to underrepresented minority students pursuing research. Dr. Laurencin is also active in addressing health disparities. Dr. Laurencin completed the Program in African American Studies at Princeton University. He is a core faculty member of the Africana Studies Institute at the University of Connecticut, and is editor-in-chief of the *Journal of Racial and Ethnic Health Disparities*, published by Springer Nature. He co-founded the W. Montague Cobb/NMA Health Institute, dedicated to addressing health disparities, and served as its founding chair. The W. Montague Cobb/NMA Health Institute and the National Medical Association established the Cato T. Laurencin Lifetime Research Achievement Award, given during the opening ceremonies of the National Medical Association Meeting. He is a recipient of the Herbert W. Nickens Award from the AAAS recognizing his work advancing social justice and equity.

Dr. Laurencin is an elected member of the National Academy of Medicine, an elected member of the National Academy of Engineering, and an elected member of the American Academy of Arts and Sciences. Active internationally, he is an elected fellow of the Indian National Academy of Sciences, the Indian National Academy of Engineering, the African Academy of Sciences, and the World Academy of Sciences, and is an academician of the Chinese Academy of Engineering.

Dr. Laurencin is the recipient of the National Medal of Technology and Innovation, America's highest honor for technological achievement, awarded by President Barack Obama in ceremonies at the White House. He is the first individual in history to receive the oldest/highest award of the National Academy of Medicine (the Walsh McDermott Medal) and the oldest/highest award of the National Academy of Engineering (the Simon Ramo Founders Award).

Gilda A. Barabino, Ph.D., became the second president of Olin College of Engineering, and professor of biomedical and chemical engineering, on July 1, 2020. Previously she served as dean of the Grove School of Engineering at the City College of New York (CCNY). She also served as Daniel and Frances Berg Professor, with appointments in the Departments of Biomedical Engineering and Chemical Engineering, as well as the City University of New York School of Medicine.

A biomedical engineer trained in chemical engineering, with broad interest in global health, systems, and interdisciplinary engineering education, Dr. Barabino is a noted investigator in the areas of sickle cell disease and cellular and tissue engineering. She is an internationally recognized thought leader and highly sought speaker and consultant on race/ethnicity and gender in science and engineering, with particular focus on creating cultures and climates that support a sense of belonging. She has led a number of initiatives in these areas, including serving as the founder and executive director of the National Institute for Faculty Equity.

Before joining CCNY, she served as associate chair for graduate studies and professor in the Wallace H. Coulter Department of Biomedical Engineering at Georgia Tech and Emory University. She also served as Georgia Tech's inaugural vice provost for academic diversity. Prior to that, she spent 18 years at Northeastern University, rising to the rank of full professor of chemical engineering and serving as vice provost for undergraduate education.

Dr. Barabino is an active member of the National Academy of Engineering and the National Academy of Medicine and serves on numerous committees of the National Academies of Sciences, Engineering, and Medicine, including the Committee on Women in Science, Engineering and Medicine; the Roundtable on Black Men and Black Women in Science, Engineering, and Medicine; the Underrepresentation of Women of Color in Tech Project; the Ad-Hoc Committee for the Gulf Scholars Program; the Committee on Addressing Sickle Cell Disease; and the National Institutes of Health National Institute of Biomedical Imaging and Bioengineering Strategic Planning Working Group. Dr. Barabino also serves as a member of the National Science Foundation's Advisory Committee for Engineering; the congressionally mandated Committee on Equal Opportunities in Science and Engineering; and the American Association for the Advancement of Science Committee on Science, Engineering and Public Policy. Dr. Barabino also serves on the Scientific Advisory Board of the Chan Zuckerberg Biohub.

Her many honors include the American Institute of Chemical Engineers Award for Service to Society (2019); the Presidential Award for Excellence in Science, Mathematics, and Engineering Mentoring (2018); the Pierre Galetti Award (2017), the American Institute for Medical and Biological Engineering's highest honor; and an honorary degree from Xavier University of Louisiana (2016).

She is currently the chair of the American Society of Engineering Education Engineering Deans Council. She sits on the board of trustees for VentureWell, Associated Universities, Inc., and Xavier University of Louisiana. Dr. Barabino earned her B.S. degree in chemistry from Xavier

University of Louisiana and her Ph.D. in chemical engineering from Rice University.

George Q. Daley, M.D., Ph.D., is dean and Caroline Shields Walker Professor of Medicine at Harvard Medical School. He is also professor of biological chemistry and molecular pharmacology. Prior to becoming dean, he was the director of the Pediatric Stem Cell Transplantation Program at Dana-Farber/Boston Children's Cancer and Blood Disorders Center and an investigator of the Howard Hughes Medical Institute. Dr. Daley received his A.B., magna cum laude, from Harvard University (1982); a Ph.D. in biology from the Massachusetts Institute of Technology (1989), working with Nobel laureate David Baltimore; and his M.D., summa cum laude, from Harvard Medical School (1991). Dr. Daley pursued clinical training in internal medicine at Massachusetts General Hospital, where he served as chief resident (1994–1995), and a clinical fellowship in hematology/oncology at Brigham and Women's Hospital and Children's Hospitals. He remains a staff member in pediatric hematology/oncology at Boston Children's Hospital. His research uses mouse and human disease models to study cancer and blood disorders. Dr. Daley has been elected to the National Academy of Medicine, the American Society for Clinical Investigation, the American Association of Physicians, the American Pediatric Societies, the American Academy of Arts and Sciences, and the American Association for the Advancement of Science. He was an inaugural winner of the National Institutes of Health Director's Pioneer Award (2004), and has won the E. Donnall Thomas Lecture and Prize of the American Society of Hematology. He was a founding executive committee member of the Harvard Stem Cell Institute, served as president of the International Society for Stem Cell Research (2007–2008), and anchored the special task forces that produced the society's guidelines for stem cell research and clinical translation (2006, 2008, 2016). He was on the organizing committee for both the 2015 and the 2018 International Summits on Human Genome Editing and has advocated publicly for responsible international guidelines for attempts at germline genome editing.

Theodore Corbin, M.D., M.P.P., is professor and vice chair in the Department of Emergency Medicine at the Drexel University College of Medicine (DUCOM). He also serves as the medical director of the Healing Hurt People Program, an emergency department–based, trauma-informed intervention strategy that identifies victims of intentional injury. Most recently he was appointed as the associate dean of community and external affairs at DUCOM. Dr. Corbin received his master's in public policy from the Princeton School of Public and International Affairs. Recipient of the 2017 Drexel University College of Medicine Distinguished Alumni, Dr. Corbin also codirects the Center for Nonviolence and Social Justice at Drexel University School of Public Health, where he holds a joint appointment. He was awarded a Stoneleigh Foundation Fellowship and an Annie E. Casey Foundation grant to explore the impact of PTSD (posttraumatic stress disorder) on violently injured youth and young adults, and to evaluate the effectiveness of Healing Hurt People. His work focuses broadly on addressing the trauma in the lives of victims of violence, especially boys and men of color, for whom violence is a leading cause of disability and death.

Louis W. Sullivan, M.D., is the chairman and CEO of the Sullivan Alliance to Transform the Health Professions. He is also chairman of the board of the National Health Museum in Atlanta, Georgia, which aims to improve the health of Americans by enhancing health literacy and advancing healthy behaviors. Dr. Sullivan served as chair of the President's Commission on Historically Black Colleges and Universities from 2002 to 2009 and was co-chair of the President's Commission on HIV and AIDS from 2001 to 2006. With the exception of his tenure as secretary of the Department of Health and Human Services (HHS) from 1989 to 1993, Dr. Sullivan was president of Morehouse School of Medicine for more than two decades. As secretary of HHS, Dr. Sullivan's efforts to improve the health and health behavior of Americans included (1) the introduction of a new and improved Food and Drug Administration food label; (2) release of *Healthy People 2000*, a guide for improved health promotion/disease prevention activities; (3) education of the public about health dangers from tobacco use; (4) successful efforts to prevent the introduction of "Uptown," a nonfiltered, mentholated cigarette by R.J. Reynolds Tobacco Company; (5) inauguration of a $100 million minority male health and injury prevention initiative; and (6) implementation of greater gender and ethnic diversity in senior positions of HHS, including the appointment of the first female director of the National Institutes of Health, the first female and first Hispanic surgeon general of the U.S. Public Health Service, and the first African American commissioner of the Social Security Administration.

Marc Nivet, Ed.D., M.B.A., is the executive vice president for institutional advancement at the University of Texas (UT) Southwestern Medical Center.

In this capacity, he provides strategic vision and oversight for the areas of development, communications, marketing and public affairs, government affairs, and community and corporate relations.

Prior to his role at UT Southwestern, Dr. Nivet served as a member of the executive leadership team of the Association of American Medical Colleges (AAMC), where he provided leadership on issues surrounding community engagement, diversity, and health equity at medical schools and teaching hospitals across the United States and Canada.

Prior to joining the AAMC, Dr. Nivet served as the chief operating officer and treasurer for the Josiah Macy Jr. Foundation, which fosters innovation in health professional education that aligns workforce training with the dynamic needs of patients.

Dr. Nivet has spent more than 20 years in academic medicine developing creative program initiatives and innovative approaches to advance the mission of excellence in research, education, and patient care. He earned his doctorate in higher education management from the University of Pennsylvania and his M.B.A. with a focus on health-care management from George Washington University's School of Business.

Raj Chetty, Ph.D., is the William A. Ackman Professor of Public Economics at Harvard University and director of Opportunity Insights. Dr. Chetty's research combines empirical evidence and economic theory to help design more effective government policies. His work on tax policy, unemployment insurance, and education has been widely cited in media outlets and congressional testimony. His current research focuses on equality of opportunity: How can we give children from disadvantaged backgrounds better chances of succeeding?

Dr. Chetty earned his A.B., summa cum laude, from Harvard College in 2000 and his Ph.D. from Harvard University in 2003. At the age of 23, he became a professor at the University of California, Berkeley until 2009, when he returned to Harvard as one of the youngest tenured professors in Harvard's history. Dr. Chetty was a faculty member at Stanford University from 2015 to 2018. In summer 2018, he returned to Harvard, where he rejoined the Economic Department and launched Opportunity Insights.

Dr. Chetty has received numerous awards for his research, including a MacArthur "Genius" Fellowship and the John Bates Clark Medal, given to the economist under 40 whose work is judged to have made the most significant contribution to the field. He has also received the Sherwin Rosen Prize of the Society of Labor Economists and Calvó-Armengol International

Prize in Economics. He was elected as a fellow of the American Academy of Arts and Sciences in 2014 and as a member of the National Academy of Sciences in 2018.

David Satcher, M.D., Ph.D., is a physician-scientist and public health administrator with an extensive track record of leadership, research, and community engagement. He is a Phi Beta Kappa graduate of Morehouse College and holds M.D. and Ph.D. degrees from Case Western Reserve University, were he was also elected to Alpha Omega Alpha Honor Society. Dr. Satcher served as the 16th surgeon general of the United States (1998–2002) and the 10th assistant secretary for health in the Department of Health and Human Services (1998–2001). He also served as director of the Centers for Disease Control and Prevention and administrator of the Agency for Toxic Substances and Disease Registry. Dr. Satcher has also held top leadership positions at the Charles R. Drew University for Medicine and Science, Meharry Medical College, and Morehouse School of Medicine. He has received more than 50 honorary degrees and has received numerous awards from diverse organizations and agencies. Currently, Dr. Satcher is the founding director and senior advisor for the Satcher Health Leadership Institute at the Morehouse School of Medicine, Atlanta, Georgia.

Sonsiere Cobb-Souza is the director of the Division of Program Operations for the Office of Minority Health (OMH) at the U.S. Department of Health and Human Services (HHS). She leads development and implementation of public health programs to reduce health disparities, improve quality of care, and increase the diversity of the health-related workforce, as well as policy demonstrations and initiatives that target hard-to-reach, high-risk, and disenfranchised racial and ethnic minority populations. During her more than 35-year public health career, Ms. Cobb-Souza held several progressively responsible public health positions at the local and state levels in Illinois, Ohio, and Wisconsin, and the federal level at the Centers for Disease Control and Prevention (CDC).

Prior to joining OMH, Ms. Cobb-Souza served as deputy director for the CDC Office of Minority Health and Health Disparities (OMHD) from 2002 to 2007. She also held a number of management positions at CDC, including associate director for policy, planning, and evaluation in the OMHD. Among her accomplishments at CDC, she served as an agency expert on national minority health programs, injury, and premature death affecting minority populations; led coordination of the Initiative to

Eliminate Racial and Ethnic Health Disparities; and co-led development and implementation of CDC and HHS policies and programs related to racial and ethnic health. Ms. Cobb-Souza also served as chief of the Training and Education Branch, National Immunization Program, and as lead project officer for the National Center for Prevention Services (NCPS), National Minority Organizations (NMO) HIV Prevention Programs. She served as the program representative for the first NCPS Nongovernmental HIV External Review and led the development of the NMO HIV Prevention and Community Planning Program.

Ms. Cobb-Souza has received numerous awards, including the 2017 Secretary's Award for Meritorious Service—Empowering Communities for a Healthier Nation Initiative, the 2010 Assistant Secretary's Award for Superior Service, the CDC Award for Exceptional Performance in Minority Health Services, the CDC Director's Award for Outstanding Leadership, and the Secretary's Award for Distinguished Service for achieving the Childhood Immunization Initiative vaccine coverage goals and the highest immunization levels ever recorded in the United States. Under Ms. Cobb-Souza's leadership, the Public Health Training Network also selected the National Immunization Program, Training and Education Branch to receive their Outstanding Performance Award. She also received the MetroHealth Systems Outstanding Service Award for Perinatal Network Special Projects in Cleveland, Ohio, and the Training Institute of Wisconsin Exceptional Service Award for Training Programs in the Areas of Adolescent Pregnancy Prevention and Reproductive Health.

Ms. Cobb-Souza completed her B.S. in health education and master's program in health-care administration from George Williams College in Downers Grove, Illinois.

Geoffrey Young, Ph.D., in his role as senior director of student affairs and programs at the Association of American Medical Colleges, serves as the AAMC's principal student affairs officer and lead content expert in undergraduate medical education student services. The focus areas under his leadership include admissions, student affairs, student diversity affairs, student records, and student financial aid. Dr. Young's unit also offers learners across the medical education continuum services in career planning, financial literacy, decision-making and debt management, and preparation for application and transition to medical school and residency. His team is recognized as a leader in holistic review and provides resources and services that enable medical schools and other health professions schools to apply the holistic review framework to their selection processes. Dr. Young works closely with the national leadership of the Group on Student Affairs, advising on strategic direction and of critical issues that impact undergraduate medical education, to develop and/or address national policies that yield effective practices within student services. Additionally, he works closely with the AAMC's Student Surveys Advisory Committee to improve medical education by providing reliable data and effective and timely program evaluation tools for medical schools.

Sylvester James "Jim" Gates Jr., Ph.D., is a theoretical physicist. In 2017, Dr. Gates retired from the University of Maryland and is currently the director of the Brown Theoretical Physics Center, Ford Foundation Professor of Physics, affiliate mathematics professor, and a faculty fellow, Watson Institute for International Studies & Public Affairs at Brown University. While at the University of Maryland, College Park, Dr. Gates was a University System Regents Professor, the John S. Toll Professor of Physics, the director of the String and Particle Theory Center, and affiliate professor of mathematics. He served on the President's Council of Advisors on Science and Technology, contemporaneously on the Maryland State Board of Education from 2009 to 2016, and the National Commission on Forensic Science from 2013 to 2016.

He is known for his work on supersymmetry, supergravity, and superstring theory. He received two B.S. degrees and a Ph.D. from the Massachusetts Institute of Technology, where his doctoral thesis was the institution's first on the topic of supersymmetry. In 1984, Dr. Gates coauthored *Superspace*, the first comprehensive book on supersymmetry. He is a past president of the National Society of Black Physicists and an NSBP Fellow, as well as a Fellow of the American Physical Society (APS), the American Association for the Advancement of Science, and the Institute of Physics in the United Kingdom. In 2019, he was elected to the presidential line of the APS, where he is currently serving as president-elect. He is also an elected member of the American Academy of Arts and Sciences and the American Philosophical Society. In 2013, he was elected to the National Academy of Sciences, becoming the first African American theoretical physicist so recognized in its 150-year history. President Obama awarded Dr. Gates the National Medal of Science at a White House ceremony in 2013.

From 1991 to 1993, Dr. Gates was the chair of the Department of Physics and Astronomy at Howard University and served as the founding director of the Center for the Study of Terrestrial and Extraterrestrial

Atmospheres funded by the National Aeronautics and Space Administration. His tenure also saw the inauguration of efforts leading to MHATTCAT (the Michigan/Howard/AT&T collaborative access team), to carry out research at the synchrotron at the Advanced Photon Source in 1994 supported by the Department of Energy. In 2007 and 2013, he served as the Rydell Visiting Professor at Gustavus Adolphus College. During 2015–2016, he was in residence at Dartmouth College as the Roth Distinguished Scholar.

Garth Graham, M.D., M.P.H., a cardiologist, researcher, and public health expert, joined Google as director and global head of health care and public health and head of YouTube Health. He previously served in two U.S. administrations as deputy assistant secretary for health, and was assistant dean for health policy and chief of health services research in the Department of Medicine at the University of Florida School of Medicine, president of the Aetna Foundation, and vice president and chief community health officer at CVS Health. He currently serves on several boards, including the National Heart, Lung, and Blood Institute Advisory Council; the board of the National Quality Forum; and the board of a Fortune 500 publicly traded company, Science Applications International Corp.

An elected member of the National Academy of Medicine, Dr. Garth obtained his M.D. at Yale University School of Medicine and M.P.H. at Yale School of Public Health, completed his residency in internal medicine at Massachusetts General Hospital, and was a cardiology fellow at Johns Hopkins. He holds three board certifications, including internal medicine, cardiology, and interventional cardiology.

James E. K. Hildreth, Ph.D., M.D., is the 12th president and chief executive officer of Meharry Medical College, the nation's largest private, independent historically Black academic health sciences center. Dr. Hildreth obtained a B.A. in chemistry from Harvard University and was selected as the first African American Rhodes Scholar from Arkansas. He obtained a Ph.D. in immunology from Oxford University, where his studies focused on the biology of virus-specific cytotoxic T cells. He obtained an M.D. from Johns Hopkins University School of Medicine and took a leave of absence from medical school for a postdoctoral fellowship in pharmacology at Johns Hopkins.

In 1987, Dr. Hildreth joined the Johns Hopkins School of faculty as assistant professor. He was appointed as the first associate dean for graduate studies at Johns Hopkins in 1994. In 2002, he became the first

African American in the 125-year history of Johns Hopkins School of Medicine to earn full professorship with tenure in basic sciences. In July 2005, Dr. Hildreth became director of the National Institutes of Health (NIH)–funded Center for AIDS Health Disparities Research at Meharry Medical College. In August of 2011, he became dean of the College of Biological Sciences at University of California, Davis. He was the first African American dean in the university, which was founded in 1905. He was also appointed as a tenured professor in the Department of Cellular and Molecular Biology as well as professor in the Department of Internal Medicine in the UC Davis School of Medicine.

Dr. Hildreth's research in immunology and virology, with a focus on HIV, has resulted in more than 120 publications in top journals and 11 patents. He has received numerous NIH grants to support his research, including a prestigious NIH Director's Pioneer Award. A technology developed by Dr. Hildreth was licensed by Genentech as the basis for the Food and Drug Administration (FDA)–approved drug Raptiva.

Dr. Hildreth received numerous awards for his research, commitment to diversity in medicine, biomedical research, and service to communities. His recognitions include honorary degrees, induction into the Arkansas Black Hall of Fame and the Johns Hopkins University Society of Scholars and election to the Institute of Medicine (now the National Academy of Medicine), part of the National Academies of Sciences, Engineering, and Medicine, the most prestigious biomedical and health policy advisory group in the United States.

Dr. Hildreth has led Meharry's effort to support the city of Nashville's response to the COVID-19 pandemic. He serves on the city's COVID-19 task force, and Meharry manages all of the city's COVID-19 test centers, performing as many as 18,000 tests per week. Meharry is also doing COVID-19 mobile testing at local churches. Dr. Hildreth led the effort to establish Meharry as a COVID-19 vaccine test site as part of Operation Warp Speed. He is also leading clinical research on a promising therapeutic for moderate to severe cases of COVID-19. Dr. Hildreth has emerged as a trusted leader in the fight against COVID-19 and has appeared numerous times in local and national print and broadcast media. As a trusted messenger, he is leading efforts to ensure that minorities enroll in COVID-19 vaccine trials and that they accept vaccines when they are approved and available. He has been appointed to the FDA's Vaccines and Related Products Advisory Committee that will review COVID-19 vaccine trial data and make recommendations for approval to the FDA commissioner.

Dr. Hildreth has served on numerous national advisory boards, including the Harvard University Board of Overseers. He currently serves on the Advisory Council to the NIH Director, the Veteran's Administration National Academic Affiliations Council, and the board of directors of the Association of Academic Health Centers. Dr. Hildreth serves on several other boards, including chair of the board of the St. Jude Children's Research Hospital Graduate School of Biomedical Sciences.

Garnesha Ezediaro is the lead of Bloomberg Philanthropies' Greenwood Initiative, an effort to increase intergenerational Black wealth and address systemic underinvestment in Black communities. Ms. Ezediaro is a proven leader with over a decade of experience serving as a catalyst for individual, community, and organizational growth. With a dedicated passion for transformation, she has worked across the public, private, and philanthropic sectors to design experiences, programs, and content that inspires mission-focused, human-led innovation.

Ms. Ezediaro returned to Bloomberg Philanthropies after serving as national director for Black Outreach for the Mike for Black America Campaign. Prior to the campaign, she worked in the media and technology sector, where she served in Global Leadership Development Programs at Verizon Media, partnering with a dynamic team to deliver trainings and targeted development programs for more than 11,000 employees globally. Her years of public service also include serving in strategic communications for the Government Innovation portfolio at Bloomberg Philanthropies, a unique program to support mayors and other city leaders in strengthening local governments around the world. She also served as communications director and spokesperson for New Orleans Mayor Mitch Landrieu and as director of marketing at Brick City Development Corporation in Newark, New Jersey, under the leadership of former Mayor Cory Booker.

Ms. Ezediaro received a B.A. from American University with a double undergraduate major in public communication and interdisciplinary studies: communications, law, economics, and government. She also studied at New York University's Wagner Graduate School of Public Service in Public and Nonprofit Management and holds a Certificate of Public Performance Management from Rutgers University–Newark.

Michele Lezama, M.S., M.B.A., is the president and CEO of the National Action Council for Minorities in Engineering, Inc. (NACME), a leading scholarship and research organization whose vision is "an engineering workforce that looks like America." Prior to NACME, she served as a strategist for Purdue University's nationally recognized Minority Engineering Program, and she was an employee of the University of Notre Dame in her role as executive director of the National GEM Consortium (GEM). GEM is a nonprofit dedicated to increasing the number of underrepresented individuals who pursue and receive a master's or Ph.D. in engineering or science by providing full fellowships and industry research experiences. Prior to GEM, Ms. Lezama served as executive director of the National Society of Black Engineers (NSBE). Under her leadership, NSBE received the 2003 Presidential Award for Excellence in Science, Mathematics, and Engineering Mentoring awarded by the White House's Office of Science and Technology Policy.

Prior to her university and nonprofit roles, Ms. Lezama was the director of satellite scrambling operations at HBO (Home Box Office), and as the associate director of broadcast operations and system integration at CBS (Columbia Broadcasting System). Prior to her media career, she held several engineering roles at IBM.

Ms. Lezama earned her B.S. in industrial engineering at Northeastern University (NACME Scholar) and both her M.S. in industrial engineering (GEM Fellow) and her M.B.A. in finance and accounting (Toigo Fellow) from Columbia University.

Anthony B. Iton, M.D., J.D., M.P.H., joined the California Endowment in October 2009 as senior vice president of healthy communities.

Prior to his appointment at the Endowment, Dr. Iton served since 2003 as both the director and county health officer for the Alameda County Public Health Department. In that role, he oversaw the creation of an innovative public health practice designed to eliminate health disparities by tackling the root causes of poor health that limit quality of life and lifespan in many of California's low-income communities.

Dr. Iton also served for 3 years as director of health and human services and school medical advisor for the City of Stamford, Connecticut. Concurrent to that, he also served as a physician in internal medicine for Stamford Hospital's HIV Clinic. In addition, Dr. Iton served for 5 years as a primary care physician for the San Francisco Department of Public Health.

Dr. Iton's varied career also includes past service as a staff attorney and health policy analyst for the West Coast regional office of Consumer's Union, the publisher of *Consumer Reports* magazine. He has been published in numerous public health and medical publications and is a regular public health lecturer and keynote speaker at conferences across the nation. He earned his B.S. in neurophysiology, with honors, from McGill University, in Montreal, Quebec; his J.D. at the University of California, Berkeley's Boalt Hall School of Law; and his medical degree from Johns Hopkins University School of Medicine.

Maureen Cullins, A.M., is director of the Multicultural Resource Center and associate director and senior advisor of the Masters of Biomedical Sciences Program in the Duke University School of Medicine. She has been at Duke University for 34 years, beginning her career in Student Affairs on the undergraduate campus. Ms. Cullins has been a pre-health advisor and worked with first-generation, low-wealth students for more than 20 years.

Ms. Cullins has actively advocated for marginalized students and staff of color since arriving at Duke. Her work led to the establishment of the Women's Center, Community Service Center (now the Center for Civic Engagement), and the Center for Lesbian, Gay and Transgender Life (now the Center for Sexual and Gender Diversity) in the Division of Student Affairs. She is an active member of numerous university committees, advisor to student organizations, academic advisor, lecturer, and series and conference organizer. She promotes the well-being of all members of the Duke community and provides opportunities for education on issues of race, gender, religion, and sexuality and their impact on health and health care. In the School of Medicine, she addresses the environmental issues that impact student success—social justice, affinity groups advisement, harassment prevention, pathway programs, and antidiscrimination. At this moment in U.S. history, Ms. Cullins is actively engaged with the School of Medicine in its antiracism work. She is on the steering committee for the Anti-racism in Medical Education Task Force and co-chairs the committee reviewing the policies and practices of Student Affairs. She co-leads the Leadership Accountability workgroup on the Association of American Medical College's Action Collaborative on Black Men in Medicine.

Her professional interests include languages and linguistics, adult literacy, young adult development, inter- and intragroup dynamics, dispute resolution, health disparities, and cultural competency. Ms. Cullins holds a bachelor's degree in French and anthropology from Duke University and a master's degree and advanced graduate study in linguistics from the University of Pennsylvania.

Wynter J. Duncanson, Ph.D., earned her B.S.E. in bioengineering with a minor in materials science and engineering at the University of

Pennsylvania. Upon completion of her Ph.D. at Boston University (BU) in biomedical engineering, she began a postdoc in applied physics at the Harvard Paulson School of Engineering. After her postdoc, she participated in developing a Western-style education and research system in a 3-year-old university, Nazarbayev University (NU), in Kazakhstan in Central Asia.

Through research and teaching at NU, she was able to provide unprecedented access to a research-based engineering curriculum. She worked with a few students to found the first International Affiliate Student chapter of the Society of Women Engineers in Central Asia. In her time as a lecturer at Boston University, she has been engaged in supporting students as the faculty advisor for the National Society of Black Engineers and building the graduate student pipeline through recruiting at National Affinity conferences. As the assistant dean of outreach and diversity, she is leading the College of Engineering at Boston University toward becoming a more diverse, equitable, and inclusive college for all, particularly those from traditionally underrepresented groups.

Dr. Duncanson has been actively increasing the graduate student pipeline by amplifying the college's presence at conferences serving students of underrepresented groups, and creating a prospective student database from these conferences and through databases. In addition, she has been building the faculty pipeline through hosting research symposia in which postdocs and late-stage graduate students are invited. To expand the college's impact and truly reach underrepresented populations worldwide, she has been developing partnerships with minority-serving institutions and other organizations worldwide. She has been developing partnerships with minority-serving institutions and other organizations to identify barriers inhibiting progress in inclusion.

Dr. Duncanson has become the leader of the 9 year old Boston University College of Engineering undergraduate facilitated engineering outreach program, the Technology Innovation Scholars Program. Historically, BU's undergraduates, "Inspiration Ambassadors," went into middle and high school classrooms educating and inspiring students about engineering and helping them complete mini-engineering activities, known as "Innovations in a Box." In the new post-COVID-19 world without physical classrooms, the college has expanded and refined its reach by working with elementary schools and using a blended modality of remote and in-person learning. Dr. Duncanson has been working to increase access for engineering outreach for underserved populations in the greater Boston area.

Byron Ford, Ph.D., is associate dean of pre-clerkship medical education and professor of biomedical sciences at the University of California, Riverside (UCR) School of Medicine. He was previously director of the Graduate Program in Biomedical Sciences at UCR. Dr. Ford received his B.S. degree from Grambling State University and Ph.D. from Meharry Medical College. He completed postdoctoral studies in neurobiology at Harvard Medical School and the National Institutes of Health (NIH). He was professor and vice department chair of neurobiology at the Morehouse School of Medicine before moving to UCR in 2015. Dr. Ford's laboratory has studied mechanisms of neuroprotection and inflammatory mediators in ischemic stroke for more than 20 years. He has been the recipient of NIH and Department of Defense grants to investigate the neuroprotective roles of neuregulin-1 in stroke, traumatic brain injury, and cerebral malaria and as a countermeasure for nerve agent exposure. His work has yielded nine full U.S. patents and several additional patent applications. Dr. Ford was a member of the National Institute for Neurological Disorders and Stroke Advisory Council at NIH from 2012 to 2016. He has been directly involved in the training of 10 postdoctoral fellows, 23 graduate/medical students, and more than 100 undergraduate students. In 2017, Dr. Ford received a grant from the NIH Bridges to the Baccalaureate (B2B) Program, which was established between UCR and Riverside City College (RCC) to create a research education program to facilitate transfer of diverse RCC students into science, technology, engineering, and mathematics majors. Dr. Ford received a University of California–Historically Black Colleges and Universities (UC-HBCU) Initiative grant in 2020 to improve diversity and strengthen UC graduate programs by investing in relationships between UC faculty and Morehouse College, Spelman College, the Morehouse School of Medicine, and Fort Valley State University in Georgia. Dr. Ford is also co-principal investigator of a $2.3 million Health Resources and Services Administration grant titled Agents of Change for a Healthier Tomorrow: Transformational Integration of Quality Improvement with Primary Care Education. The goal of the program is to expand and strengthen the primary care workforce and to prepare the next generation of physicians to transform health-care delivery systems in order to improve health outcomes and lower overall costs, particularly for patient populations facing health-care disparities.

Michelle McMurry-Heath, M.D., Ph.D., assumed the leadership of the Biotechnology Innovation Organization (BIO) as president and CEO on

June 1, 2020. A medical doctor and molecular immunologist by training, Dr. McMurry-Heath became just the third chief executive to steward the world's largest biotechnology advocacy group since BIO's founding in 1993.

BIO represents 1,000 life sciences companies and organizations from 30 countries. The organization's mission is to support companies that discover and deploy scientific breakthroughs that improve human health, environmental stewardship, and sustainable agriculture. The common thread in Dr. McMurry-Heath's work across academia, government, and industry has been her focus on broadening access to scientific progress so that more patients from diverse backgrounds can benefit from cutting-edge innovation. Driven by her own past family experiences navigating clinical trials and funding uncertainties within the rare disease community, she calls "the distribution of scientific progress the social justice issue of our age."

Dr. McMurry-Heath came to BIO from Johnson & Johnson, where she served as global head of evidence generation for medical device companies and then vice president of global external innovation and global leader for regulatory sciences. She was also instrumental in bringing Johnson & Johnson's incubator, JLabs, to Washington, D.C. She led a team of 900 with responsibilities in 150 countries around the globe.

Prior to her time at Johnson & Johnson, Dr. McMurry-Heath was also a key science policy leader in government. The Obama-Biden transition team tapped her to conduct a comprehensive analysis of the National Science Foundation's policies, programs, and personnel. President Obama then named her associate science director of the Food and Drug Administration's Center for Devices and Radiological Health under Commissioner Peggy Hamburg. In that role, she championed clinical trial evolution, the use of real-world evidence in product evaluation, and an embrace of the patient's voice in health research so that new medical products deliver outcomes that matter to them. Dr. McMurry-Heath was the founding director of the Aspen Institute's Health, Biomedical Science, and Society Policy Program, where she promoted personalized medicine and bolstered international preparation for pandemic disease threats. She received her early training in science policy from the Robert Wood Johnson Foundation and later served as Senator Joe Lieberman's top legislative aide for science and health. In that role, she drafted legislation to protect the country from biological attacks.

Dr. McMurry-Heath received her M.D./Ph.D. from Duke's Medical Scientist Training Program, becoming the first African American to graduate from the prestigious program. She spent 12 years working at the research bench before taking policy and leadership roles in government and industry.